It's another great book from CGP...

You can't escape from English — it's everywhere.
You can't escape from English GCSEs either... and they can be a real challenge.

Not to worry. This brilliant CGP Revision Guide clearly explains everything
you'll need for success in GCSE English Language <u>and</u> English Literature
— all fully up to date for the latest Grade 9-1 courses.

We've included example answers that show you how to tackle exam questions,
plus unbeatable advice on how to score top marks in the real GCSEs.
Plenty of prose, no cons.

CGP — still the best! ☺

Our sole aim here at CGP is to produce the highest quality books —
carefully written, immaculately presented and dangerously close to being funny.

Then we work our socks off to get them out to you
— at the cheapest possible prices.

CONTENTS

CONTENTS

CONTENTS

Section Eleven — Spelling, Punctuation and Grammar

Section Twelve — Spoken Language Assessment

Published by CGP

Editors: Claire Boulter, Louise Taylor, Matt Topping

With thanks to Holly Poynton for the proofreading.
With thanks to Laura Jakubowski for the copyright research.

Acknowledgements:
With thanks to iStockPhoto.com for permission to use the images on pages 1, 31, 47, 60, 66, 67, 78 and 84.
'Ghosts' by Robert W. Service, by courtesy of Mrs Anne Longepe.

Every effort has been made to locate copyright holders and obtain permission to reproduce sources. For those sources where it has been difficult to trace the copyright holder of the work, we would be grateful for information. If any copyright holder would like us to make an amendment to the acknowledgements, please notify us and we will gladly update the book at the next reprint. Thank you.

ISBN: 978 1 78294 366 2
Printed by Elanders Ltd, Newcastle upon Tyne.
Clipart from Corel®

Based on the classic CGP style created by Richard Parsons.

Text, design, layout and original illustrations © Coordination Group Publications Ltd. (CGP) 2015

How To Use This Book

GCSE English exams — yep, they're on their way. This book tells you what to expect from your English Language and English Literature exams, and how to deal with even the trickiest questions the exam boards throw at you.

Check whether you're doing one English GCSE or two

1) Everybody has to study English Language at GCSE. Page 6 tells you more about what you'll have to do in the exam, and what the examiners will be looking for in your answers.

2) You might also take a GCSE in English Literature. If you do, you'll have to read and analyse a range of prose, drama and poetry — page 36 gives you more information on what you'll study and what you need to do to get a great mark in the exam.

Learn how to write great exam answers

1) Section One of this book gives you advice on how to plan and write answers for English Language and English Literature. It includes extracts from sample answers to show you how to approach the different types of questions you're likely to come across.

2) Accurate grammar, punctuation and spelling is vital — you can pick up extra marks for writing well in both English Language and English Literature. Section Eleven, near the end of the book, gives you loads of tips on how to make sure your answers are accurate and well written.

Dani liked to approach the question with stealth.

© iStockphoto.com/MAEK123

3) To get a top grade, you need to know the correct technical terms (rhetoric, alliteration, stanza etc). There's a handy glossary at the back of the book that defines all the terms you'll need.

Get to grips with the English Language course

1) Sections Two to Four of this book are about English Language:

- Section Two is all about how to read, understand and select information from the different types of texts that might come up in the exams.

- Section Three digs deeper into the techniques that writers use — it shows you how to pick out different features of language and structure and analyse their effects.

- Section Four guides you through how to write your own creative and non-fiction texts — it gives you advice on how to structure your writing, the sort of things to include and what language to use.

2) You'll also be assessed on your spoken language, but this won't count towards your GCSE. Section Twelve gives you some pointers on how to do well in the spoken language assessment.

Get ready for the English Literature exams

There's no replacement for knowing your set texts really well, but Sections Five to Ten of this book will give you a helping hand to get a top grade in your English Literature exams:

- Section Five gives you advice on what to look out for when you're studying a prose or drama text.

- Section Six is all about the specific things you need to think about if you're reading a play, and Section Seven covers the different elements of prose texts.

- Section Eight talks you through analysing poetry, including how to compare poems.

- Section Nine shows you how to get to grips with the poems in your Poetry Anthology, and Section Ten is all about how to understand and analyse a poem you haven't read before.

Planning Your Answers

We've all been there — you turn over your exam paper, read the question, notice that time's slipping away and start desperately scribbling your answer. But I promise, if you take a few minutes to plan, you won't regret it.

Read the questions carefully and calmly

1) Give yourself time to read through the questions and any texts or extracts at the start of the exam.

2) Always read the questions before the texts or extracts — that way, you'll know what to look out for.

3) Make sure you're clear about what the questions are asking you to do by underlining the key words.

> How does Brontë present the changing relationship between Jane and Mr Rochester?

4) Once you've read the questions, carefully read though any texts or extracts you've been given. It's a good idea to highlight key words or phrases that will help you to answer the questions — but don't spend ages doing this.

Remember, it's your exam paper and you can write on it if it helps you.

Jot down your main ideas before you start writing

1) You don't need to make a plan for short-answer questions.

2) For each long-answer question (e.g. those that require you to write an essay or a piece of descriptive writing), spend a few minutes planning your answer.

3) Don't go into too much detail — just get your main ideas down, and outline the structure of your answer.

> 'Modern music glorifies violent and criminal lifestyles and should be banned.'
>
> Write a speech, to be delivered in your school assembly, in which you explain your point of view on this statement.
>
> PLAN
>
> Para 1 — Intro
>
> "My fellow students" etc, don't listen to critics - we're currently in a golden era of music.
>
> Para 2 — Not all modern music glorifies violence - give examples.
>
> Para 3 — It's not just modern music - old music did this too. Give examples.
>
> Para 4 — People aren't robots - won't just become violent by listening to music.
>
> Para 5 — Ban = bad for freedom of expression. Censorship. Slippery slope etc.
>
> Para 6 — Conc
>
> Critics = out of touch. Haven't really listened to much 'modern music'.
>
> Modern music = celebration of choice.

Make sure your points are linked to the question — think about purpose, form and audience.

Make sure you're clear about which side you're arguing for before you start.

Briefly outline the focus of each paragraph.

To save time, write in note form.

A plan is like a nice hot water bottle...

... useful and comforting when you need it, but you don't need it all the time. You won't need to plan for every question, but it's a good idea to make a brief plan to help you tackle some of the longer answers.

P.E.E.D.

You can have loads of great ideas in your answers, but you won't get good marks unless you explain and develop them properly. That's where P.E.E.D. comes in — use it wisely, my young apprentice...

P.E.E.D. stands for Point, Example, Explain, Develop

To write good English essays about texts you've read, you must do <u>four</u> things:

1) Make a <u>point</u> to answer the question you've been given.

2) Then give an <u>example</u> from the text (see page 4 for more on this).

3) After that, <u>explain</u> how your example backs up your point.

4) Finally, <u>develop</u> your point — this might involve saying what the <u>effect on the reader</u> is, saying what the <u>writer's intention</u> is, <u>linking</u> your point to another part of the text or giving your <u>own opinion</u>.

"That wasn't really the kind of back up I was thinking of..." thought Sergeant Beker.

The <u>explanation</u> and <u>development</u> parts are very important. They're your chance to show that you <u>really understand</u> and have <u>thought about</u> the text. Here are a couple of <u>examples</u>:

How does the writer use language to show how she feels about school dinners?

This is your <u>point</u>. → The writer feels quite angry about school dinners. She says school food is "pallid, tasteless pap". ← This is your <u>example</u>.

The word "pap" has a disgusted sound to it. It emphasises how appalled she is at the ← This bit is your <u>explanation</u>.

low quality of the food. I think the writer's intention is to show

This is where you <u>develop</u> your point further. → that it isn't surprising that school dinners are unpopular. She is implying that schools should provide food that isn't disgusting if they want children to eat it.

How does Shakespeare present Lady Macbeth's attitude to power?

This introduces the main <u>point</u> of the paragraph. → Shakespeare presents Lady Macbeth as even more obsessed with power than Macbeth himself. She calls Macbeth a "coward" and says that he ← Quotes are used as the <u>example</u> here.

This <u>explains</u> the effect of the example. → "dare not" murder Duncan in order to become king. Manipulating him to commit a terrible crime shows how desperate she is for Macbeth to attain

power so that she can rule alongside him. In Shakespeare's day, women were seen as gentler and less ambitious than men, so Lady Macbeth's quest for power would have shocked an audience of the time. ← This <u>develops</u> the point by relating it to context.

Would you like to share the joke with the rest of the class?

There are other versions of P.E.E.D., but they all mean similar things — P.E.E.R. (Point, Example, Explain, Relate), P.E.E.C.E. (Point, Example, Explain, Compare, Explore). I just chose P.E.E.D. because it tickles me...

Using Examples

However fabulous the point you make in your answer is, it won't get you top marks unless you can back it up with examples from the text. Cue a page that shows you how it's done...

Use details from the text to back up your points

Whenever you make a <u>point</u> about a text, you need to use short pieces of <u>evidence</u> to <u>back it up</u>.

Summarise the woman's treatment of her pets.

The woman was cruel to her dog.

This answer doesn't give any evidence.

This is much better — it gives examples to back up the point.

The woman was cruel to her dog: she kept him chained up in the sun all day with very little food and no water.

Your evidence can be quotes or examples

1) Your evidence could be a <u>quote</u> from the text. If you use a quote, keep it <u>short</u>. It'll really impress the examiner if you <u>embed</u> it in a sentence, like this:

The writer refers to the situation as "indefensible", suggesting that he is extremely critical of the way it has been handled.

Using short embedded quotes like this lets you combine the 'example' and 'explain' parts of P.E.E.D. (see p.3) in one sentence.

2) <u>Paraphrased details</u> from the text also work well as examples. You just need to describe one of the <u>writer's techniques</u>, or one of the <u>text's features</u>, in your own words, like this:

Tennyson uses a rhetorical question in the final stanza, which emphasises the heroism of the Light Brigade.

3) Here's an <u>example</u> to show you how to work your evidence into your answer:

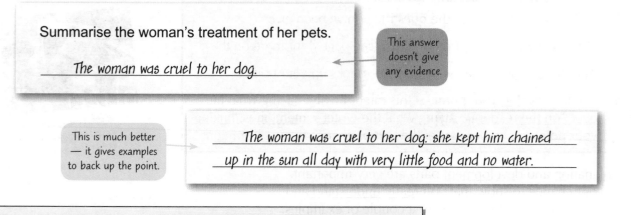

Compare the two writers' attitudes to international travel and how they put across these attitudes.

The author of source B has a very negative attitude towards international travel. In her opening paragraph, she uses a long sentence that is packed with negative verbs and adjectives, including "delayed" and "dreary", to convey the hassle of long-distance travelling and to make the reader feel weary. By contrast, the author of source A demonstrates a much more positive attitude, opening her letter with the short but decisive sentence, "The journey was a perfect joy!" which sounds energetic and cheerful.

You can use quotes and examples from the text.

Embedding short quotes will help your answer to flow smoothly.

If you need to use a longer quote, make sure you copy it correctly and use the correct punctuation.

The author's negative attitude to revision is shown by frequent sighs...

You'll definitely improve your grade if you put loads of good examples and quotes into your answers. And you can... quote... me on that. Ha ha. I don't know why my stand-up career failed so tragically.

Reading With Insight

To get the top grades, you need to show that you can 'read with insight' — you've got to make it clear that you've thought about more than just the surface meaning of the text. Think of it as detective work, my dear Watson...

You need to look beyond what's obvious

Picking out hidden meanings will help you to make sure you've done the 'D' part of P.E.E.D. — look back at p.3 for more on this.

1) You may understand what <u>happens</u> in a text, or what it's <u>about</u>, but you'll need to write about <u>more</u> than just that in your answers.

2) You can show <u>insight</u> if you work out what the writer's <u>intentions</u> are and how they want the reader to <u>feel</u>.

3) Here are a couple of <u>examples</u> of the kinds of things you could write:

The rhetorical questions make the reader doubt whether homework is a good thing. The writer seems to want to make readers feel guilty. ➡ Think about the reasons <u>why</u> the writer has included certain features — show you've understood their <u>intended effect</u> on the reader.

There is a strong sense that the writer is suffering after the loss of his friend. Perhaps the writer felt he needed to make sure the memory of his friend was kept alive. ➡ You could comment on the writer's <u>attitude</u> and <u>why</u> you think they chose to write the piece.

4) Remember to include <u>examples</u> from the text to <u>support</u> your interpretation:

Darcy is portrayed as an unlikeable character in this extract. He is described as "above being pleased", hinting at his arrogance and haughtiness. However, the swiftness with which the ball-goers change their opinion of him shows their fickleness and hints that their judgement is not to be trusted. ➡ Try to explain <u>how</u> the writer creates a particular impression of a character or event. Examiners love it if you can give <u>alternative interpretations</u> that go beyond the obvious.

Inference means working things out from clues

1) Writers don't usually make things obvious — but you can use <u>evidence</u> from the text to make an <u>inference</u> about what the writer <u>really</u> wants us to think.

2) You need to analyse <u>details</u> from the text to show what they <u>reveal</u> about the writer's intentions:

The writer uses words like "endless" and "unoriginal", which imply that he did not enjoy the film. ➡ The writer's <u>language</u> indicates their <u>emotions</u> and <u>attitude</u>.

The writer sounds sarcastic when she calls the contestants "the finest brains the country could scrape together". ➡ The writer will often use <u>tone</u> (see page 13) to <u>imply</u> what they really mean — look out for <u>sarcasm</u> (see page 17) or <u>bias</u> (see page 18).

3) You could use <u>phrases</u> like these to show that you've made an <u>inference</u>:

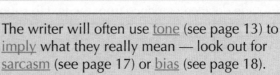

The writer gives a sense of...   The writer appears to be...   This suggests that...

Make sure you're reading with insight of a cup of tea...

Keep an eye out for any clues that might reveal how the writer has crafted their text to have a particular effect on the reader — they've certainly got a few tricks up their sleeves, these pesky writers.

Introduction to English Language

This page tells you what to expect from your English Language exams, so when the time comes they won't be as scary as you think. Sections Two, Three and Four cover what you'll have to do in more detail.

GCSE English Language assesses your reading and writing

1) English Language is a compulsory GCSE — everyone has to do it.

2) The English Language GCSE is designed to test your reading skills. In the exams you'll probably have to:

- read and answer questions on two non-fiction texts you haven't studied before. The two texts will be from different centuries (e.g. one from the 19th century and one from the 21st century).

- read and answer questions on one or two fiction texts you haven't studied before.

Sections Two and Three of this book tell you how to pick out information and analyse texts.

3) You'll also be tested on your writing skills. In the exams you'll probably have to:

- write your own piece of non-fiction — e.g. an informative newspaper article or a persuasive speech.

- do some creative writing — e.g. a short story or description.

Section Four of this book gives you advice on how to write a range of text types.

4) Your speaking and listening will also be assessed, but this won't count towards your GCSE. See pages 84-85.

Each assessment objective refers to a different skill

The assessment objectives are the things you need to do to get good marks in the exam — they're the same for all exam boards. Here's a brief description of the English Language assessment objectives (AOs):

AO 1
- Pick out and understand pieces of explicit and implicit information from the texts.
- Collect and put together information from different texts.

AO 2
- Explain how writers use language and structure to achieve their purpose and influence readers.
- Use technical terms to support your analysis of language and structure.

AO 3
- Identify different writers' ideas and perspectives.
- Compare the methods used by different writers to convey their ideas.

AO 4
- Critically evaluate texts, giving a personal opinion about how successful the writing is.
- Provide detailed evidence from the text to support your opinion.

AO 5
- Write clearly and imaginatively, adapting your tone and style for various purposes and audiences.
- Organise your writing into a clear structure.

AO 6
- Use a range of sentence structures and vocabulary, so that your writing is clear and purposeful.
- Write accurately, paying particular attention to spelling, punctuation and grammar.

"How did you find the exam?" "It was just on the table..."

Don't worry if all this seems a bit overwhelming — the key is to know what you have to do, then get lots of practice at doing it. That way, when the exam comes round, answering the questions will be second nature.

Information and Ideas

Reading's no challenge — I've been doing it for years... What's that? I also have to find and summarise information? Yikes — if only someone would make a handy revision guide page telling me how...

Information and ideas can be explicit or implicit

The information in Sections Two, Three and Four is all about English Language. English Literature is covered in Sections Five to Ten.

1) The first thing you need to be able to do in order to <u>analyse</u> a text is to <u>understand</u> the basic things it's <u>telling you</u>.

2) The information and ideas you need to pick out will either be <u>explicit</u> or <u>implicit</u>.

3) <u>Explicit</u> information is <u>clearly written</u> in the text.

> *Last weekend, it rained a lot.* ⟶ The text states that it rained, so we <u>know</u> that it rained. We also know <u>how much</u> it rained — "a lot."

4) <u>Implicit</u> information needs a little more <u>detective work</u> — you need to work it out from what is said in the text.

> *The castle was dark, decrepit and freezing cold.* ⟶ In this sentence, it is <u>implied</u> that the author doesn't like the castle very much, but this isn't stated outright.

You need to be able to summarise information

1) You might be asked to pick out information and ideas on the <u>same topic</u> from two <u>different texts</u> and to <u>summarise</u> the <u>similarities</u> or <u>differences</u> in what you've picked out.

> **Source A**
>
> *What a miserable afternoon. Daddy shouted at me just for being late to school. "You should be more responsible now you're thirteen, Andrew!" he yelled. He said he had half a mind to stop wasting his money on my private education. I know he's angry, but I think it was a bit of an overreaction.*
>
> Look for <u>explicit</u> differences, such as the boys' ages...
>
> **Source B**
>
> *Today was not a happy day, even though it was Richard's 16th birthday party. Richard sat quietly, his hands folded in his lap, as Father ranted about how the party was a waste of the little money we have. Richard only broke his silence to acknowledge Father's tirade with a respectful "Yes, Sir".*
>
> ...and <u>implicit</u> differences, such as what the boys' reactions tell you about their personalities and attitudes.

2) Make sure you <u>back up</u> your points with examples from the text.

3) Use <u>linking words</u> to write about similarities and differences — they show that you've made a <u>comparison</u>.

To show similarities:
- Similarly
- Likewise
- Equally
- Also

To show differences:
- Whereas
- Although
- However
- But

These are a few examples of linking words, but there are plenty more.

It's really no scarier than an elaborate game of spot the difference...

You'll need to sharpen up your observation skills when you're finding information in texts — comment on the explicit differences between each text, but don't forget to dig a bit deeper and write about implicit ideas too.

Audience

In the exams, you'll need to think about the audience — the intended readers of the text.

Writers aim their work at general or specific audiences

1) The writer will always have a <u>group of people</u> in mind when they write — this is their <u>audience</u>.

2) The audience of a text can be quite <u>general</u>, e.g. adults, or more <u>specific</u>, e.g. parents with children under the age of 3.

3) Some texts will have <u>more than one</u> audience, e.g. children's books will try to appeal to the <u>kids</u> who read them, but also to the <u>parents</u> who will <u>buy</u> them.

How about this one, Jonny? 'Dictionary' by Colin English. Sounds like a ripping yarn.

Look for clues about the target audience

1) Sometimes you can work out <u>who</u> the target audience is by the text's <u>content</u> (subject matter):

> *This latest model is a beautiful car. Its impressive engine can send you shooting from 0-60 mph in less than 8 seconds.* ⟹ This text is clearly aimed at someone who's interested in <u>high-performance cars</u>.

2) The <u>vocabulary</u> (choice of words) can tell you about the target audience, e.g. about the <u>age group</u>:

> *Today, we witnessed a discussion on fox hunting. As one can imagine, this issue, although it has been debated for many years, still managed to elicit mixed emotions from all concerned.* ⟹ The <u>sophisticated vocabulary</u>, like 'elicit', rather than 'bring out', and the <u>complex sentences</u> show that this text is aimed at <u>adults</u>.

> *Dungeon Killer 3 is the hottest new game of the year! There are 52 awesome levels and 6 cool new characters — don't miss out on the wildest gaming experience of your life!* ⟹ This one uses modern <u>slang</u> and <u>simple sentences</u>, so it's clear that this text is aimed at <u>younger people</u>.

3) The <u>language</u> can also give you clues about the target audience's <u>level of understanding</u>:

> *The object of a game of football is to get the ball in the opposing team's goal. Sounds easy, but the other team has the same thing in mind. Also, there are eleven players on the other team trying to stop you.* ⟹ The <u>simple</u>, <u>general</u> explanations in this text show that it's written for people who <u>don't know much</u> about football.

> *The next hole was a par 3 and I hit my tee shot directly onto the green. Sadly, my putting let me down badly, and I ended up getting a bogey.* ⟹ The <u>technical vocabulary</u> here shows that this is for people who know <u>quite a bit</u> about golf.

And now we'll take any questions from the audience...

You need to work out who the intended audience of a text is so that you can discuss the writer's purpose, the techniques they use and how successful they are. Keep the target audience in mind throughout your answer.

Purpose and Viewpoint

Writers rarely write something just for the benefit of their health. Unless it's a letter to their doctor...

There are four common purposes of writing

Pages 10-11 tell you how to spot a text's purpose.

1) The <u>purpose</u> of a text is the <u>reason</u> that it's been written — what the writer is <u>trying to do</u>.

2) Most texts are written for <u>one</u> of these reasons:

To Argue or Persuade
- They give the writer's <u>opinion</u>.
- They get the reader to <u>agree</u> with them.

To Advise
- They <u>help</u> the reader to <u>do something</u>.
- They give <u>instructions</u> on what to do.

To Inform
- They <u>tell</u> the reader about something.
- They help the reader to increase their <u>understanding</u> of a subject.

To Entertain
- They are <u>enjoyable</u> to read.
- They make the reader <u>feel</u> something.

3) Lots of texts have <u>more than one</u> purpose, though. E.g. a biographical text could be written to both <u>inform</u> and <u>entertain</u> its audience.

4) In the exams, read the texts carefully and make sure that you think about <u>what</u> the writers are trying to <u>achieve</u> (and <u>how</u> they're achieving it).

5) Look out for helpful exam questions that actually <u>tell you</u> the writer's purpose. E.g. if the question asks you about how the writer uses language to <u>influence</u> the reader, you know it's about <u>persuading</u>.

Viewpoint is different to purpose

1) A writer's purpose is what they're trying to <u>do</u>, but their <u>viewpoint</u> (or attitude) is what they <u>think</u> about the <u>topics</u> that they're writing about.

2) You can work out what a writer's viewpoint might be by looking for clues in the <u>language</u>, <u>tone</u>, <u>style</u> and <u>content</u> of a text. For example:

I urge you to visit this truly unique and hidden valley — you must see such beautiful scenery at least once in your life.

This text's <u>purpose</u> is to <u>persuade</u> its audience to visit a place. The <u>author's viewpoint</u> is their <u>belief</u> that the valley is beautiful and that it should be visited. The writer uses <u>emotive adjectives</u> and an <u>upbeat tone</u> to convey their viewpoint.

Labradoodles were initially bred as guide dogs for people with allergies due to their low-shedding coats. Their gentle temperament also makes them suitable as family pets.
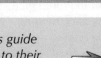
This text's <u>purpose</u> is to <u>inform</u> the audience about Labradoodles. The <u>author's viewpoint</u> is their <u>belief</u> that Labradoodles make good pets. The writer uses <u>positive adjectives</u> to convey their viewpoint.

This page was no accident — I wrote it on purpose...

So purpose can be a little harder to figure out than you'd think. If there's more than one purpose to a text, write about them both. And if you can write about how one purpose is used to achieve another, even better.

Informative and Entertaining Texts

I don't want to blow your mind or anything, but this subheading about informative texts is *itself* an informative text. Sadly, I can't promise as much for the subheading on entertaining texts...

Informative writing tells you something

1) When writing an informative text, the writer's aim is to pass on <u>knowledge</u> to the reader as <u>clearly</u> and <u>effectively</u> as possible.

Have a look back at p.8 for more on audience.

2) They will adapt their <u>language</u> to match their intended <u>audience</u>, e.g. they <u>might</u> need to write for different <u>age groups</u>, or for people with different <u>levels of understanding</u>.

3) Purely informative texts will present information in a <u>balanced</u> and <u>factual</u> way. They will contain lots of <u>facts</u> and <u>figures</u>, but no <u>opinions</u>.

The Mini first went on sale in 1959 and is widely regarded as a great icon of British culture. Soon after its release, the Mini became the bestselling car in Europe. Over five million of them were made and many famous people, including The Beatles, bought them.

→ Informative texts often contain <u>facts</u> such as dates and statistics, and use <u>clear</u>, <u>direct</u> <u>language</u> and a <u>formal</u> tone.

4) Some informative texts might also be <u>arguing</u> a particular viewpoint, though. For example:

Many newspapers <u>carefully pick</u> information that supports a particular political party. Even though a newspaper article may not say outright what its opinion is, it can still be <u>biased</u>.

Bias is when a piece of writing is influenced by the opinion of its author — see page 18.

Entertaining writing aims to be enjoyable to read

1) Entertaining writing is the sort of thing you'd read for <u>pleasure</u>, e.g. literary fiction.

2) Unlike informative texts, they contain <u>few facts</u>. Instead, they try to make you <u>feel</u> something, like <u>scared</u>, <u>excited</u>, or <u>amused</u>.

3) Entertaining writing is often very <u>descriptive</u>, and uses <u>narrative</u> <u>techniques</u> to make texts more enjoyable to read (see page 19).

4) Writers also use <u>structural techniques</u> to create entertaining texts (see pages 20 and 21). E.g. lots of <u>short</u>, <u>punchy</u> sentences can be used to make a text feel more <u>exciting</u>.

Tony's bank statement was lacking in entertaining passages.

He could feel the power of the bike humming beneath him as they both hurtled along. They were an elegant couple skimming the dance floor, whirling past plodding onlookers in their graceless cars, twisting around sharp bends with effortless precision, flying along endless straights towards the inevitable conclusion. The bike hit the wall with all its force.

→ Texts written to entertain often use <u>imagery</u> and <u>interesting vocabulary</u>, and <u>sentence lengths</u> tend to vary.

5) Writers might use entertaining writing to <u>engage</u> a reader when they have <u>another</u> purpose in mind. E.g. travel books are <u>entertaining non-fiction</u>, which are also <u>informative</u>.

I'm informative and entertaining — at least according to my CV...

It's not enough just to be able to recognise informative and entertaining writing — you also need to be able to explain how it's being used and what effect it has on the reader. If in doubt, think about how it makes you feel.

Texts that Argue, Persuade or Advise

So many texts are written to argue. If you want my advice, I think we should persuade them all to just get along. And now that I've thoroughly confused myself, here's a page to make it all crystal clear...

Arguing and persuading are similar

1) When people write to <u>argue</u>, they want to make the reader <u>agree</u> with their <u>opinion</u>. They use <u>clear</u> and <u>forceful</u> language to get their points across, and they might use <u>facts and figures</u> to back up points.

2) <u>Persuasive</u> writing tries to get the reader to <u>do something</u>, such as support a charity. It does this with techniques such as <u>emotive language</u> that aim to make the reader <u>sympathise</u> with the writer's cause.

3) When writing to <u>persuade</u>, writers might be <u>more sneaky</u> about their aims and opinions. For example:

> *It is clear that this is a good school, and that people who attend it do well.*

⟹ This writer uses the phrase 'It is clear' to make their <u>opinion</u> sound like <u>fact</u>. This can make the writing sound more <u>informative</u>, when actually it's <u>persuasive</u>.

4) When writing to argue or persuade, writers often use <u>rhetorical devices</u> such as <u>hyperbole</u> (see p.16), <u>repetition</u> or <u>rhetorical questions</u> (see p.18).

> *Eating breakfast improves mental and physical performance. This is a well-known and incontrovertible fact. And yet 20 million of us Britons regularly skip this essential refuelling opportunity. Why is this the case? Are we too busy commuting, getting the kids ready for school, blow-drying our hair? Do you often feel frantic and harassed in the morning? Well, the time has come to change.*

⟹ The writer uses <u>forceful statements</u>, <u>rhetorical questions</u>, and <u>facts and figures</u> to back up their argument. They also address the reader <u>directly</u> as 'you'.

Writing to advise sounds clear and calm

1) When writing to <u>advise</u>, writers want their readers to <u>follow their suggestions</u>.

2) The tone will be <u>calm</u> and <u>less emotional</u> than writing that argues or persuades.

3) The advice will usually be <u>clear</u> and <u>direct</u>. For example, it might use:

- <u>Vocabulary</u> that matches the audience's <u>subject knowledge</u>.
- <u>Second person</u> pronouns (e.g. 'you') to make the advice feel <u>personal</u>.
- A <u>logical structure</u> that makes the advice <u>easy to follow</u>.

All Jemima needed was some clear advice from her stylist.

4) The register (see p.13) may be <u>formal</u>, e.g. in a letter from a solicitor offering legal advice, or <u>informal</u>, e.g. in a magazine advice column.

> *Before you buy into a pension, you need to be sure that it's the right one for you — dropping out can mean that you lose a lot of the money you've already paid in.*
>
> *You should look at the pension company's reputation, past results and penalties for changing schemes. It might sound scary, but don't worry, you'll find the right one for you.*

⟹ This writer addresses the reader <u>directly</u> as 'you', uses <u>specific details</u> to give practical advice, and <u>reassures</u> the reader.

If you want my advice, I'd read this page a couple of times...

Any of these text types can be written for different audiences, but they'll always contain some of the typical features. Look for forceful statements in persuasive writing and clear, unemotional tips in writing that advises.

19th-Century Texts

In the exam, you might have to answer some questions about a 19th-century text. Chances are you weren't around in those days, so this page should have some pretty useful information for you.

19th-century writing is often quite formal

In the exam, any words in the text that aren't used today will be defined for you in a glossary.

1) 19th-century texts can sound a bit different to more modern texts, but you should still be able to understand what's going on.

2) A lot of the texts will use a more formal register (see p.13) than modern writing, even if the audience is quite familiar.

3) The sentences may be quite long and the word order can sometimes be different to modern texts. Try not to worry about this — just re-read any sentences you can't make sense of at first. Here are a couple of examples:

Then, Albert being gone and we two left alone, Edward enquired as to whether I might accompany him on a stroll in the garden.

⟹ This sentence is written using a formal register, e.g. it uses 'enquired' instead of 'asked'. It might seem a bit confusingly phrased too, but 'Albert being gone and we two left alone' is just another way of saying 'Albert had gone and the two of us were left alone.'

I believe it necessary to abandon this foul enterprise.

⟹ Sometimes it can seem as if a word has been missed out — modern writers would probably put 'is' after 'it' in this sentence.

19th-century society was different to today

1) Knowing about 19th-century society will help you to understand texts from the period better.

2) It will also help you to compare the viewpoints and perspectives of writers from different time periods.

Social Class

- Early 19th-century society was divided between the rich upper classes (who owned the land) and the poorer working classes.
- Throughout the 19th century, the Industrial Revolution was creating opportunities for more people to make more money.
- This meant that the middle class grew in size and influence throughout the century.

Education

- In the early 19th century, few children went to school. Children from poor families often worked to help support their families instead.
- In the late 19th century, education reforms made school compulsory for all young children.
- Rich families often sent their children to boarding school or hired a governess to teach them at home.

Women

- After they got married, most women were expected to look after the home and children.
- Women couldn't vote in elections. They often didn't control their own money or property.

Religion

- Christianity was influential — most of the middle and upper classes attended church regularly.
- However, science was starting to challenge some religious ideas, e.g. Darwin's theory of evolution questioned the Bible's account of creation.

19th-century texts — unlikely to contain any emojis...

It's important to get your head around the differences between 19th-century texts and more modern ones. It might feel a bit like History instead of English, but including this stuff will really improve some of your answers.

Tone and Style

No fashion tips here I'm afraid — this page is all about how writers use language in different types of writing.

Tone is the general feeling created by the text

1) A writer's tone is the <u>feeling</u> the words are written with, which creates a particular <u>mood</u> and shows what the writer's <u>attitude</u> is. For example, the tone of a text might be:

- happy or sad
- serious or funny
- sombre or light-hearted
- emotional and passionate or cool and logical

Think of a writer's tone as being like someone's tone of voice when they're talking.

2) The main way to identify a text's tone is by looking at the <u>language</u>. For example, if a writer has used <u>informal</u> language, the tone might be quite <u>personal</u> or <u>familiar</u>, but <u>formal</u> language would suggest a more <u>serious</u> or <u>distant</u> tone.

3) <u>Punctuation</u> can also give you a clue about tone. For example, if there are lots of exclamation marks, that might suggest that the tone is very <u>emotional</u> or <u>passionate</u>.

4) Tone can reflect the <u>purpose</u> of a text (e.g. informative texts often have a serious tone) or the <u>audience</u> (e.g. a playful tone might suggest a younger audience).

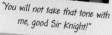
"You will not take that tone with me, good Sir Knight!"

Phillipa stood on the cold, dark street, peering up at the abandoned hotel. Despite her misgivings, she pushed tentatively on the front door, and it opened with an arthritic creak.	This passage has a <u>sinister</u> tone, which grips the reader. Adjectives ("cold, dark", "abandoned") and an adverb ("tentatively") help create the sense of <u>foreboding</u>.

Style is how the text is written

1) A text's <u>style</u> is the overall way in which it's written, which includes <u>language choices</u>, <u>sentence forms</u> and <u>structure</u>.

2) There are lots of <u>different styles</u> you might encounter. E.g. <u>cinematic</u>, where the text is written as if the reader is watching a film, or <u>journalistic</u> which is a balanced way of writing reported news.

3) <u>Register</u> is the specific language (choice of words) used to match the writing to the <u>social situation</u> that it's for. Different situations require <u>different</u> registers, for example:

Register can be thought of as a part of style.

If you wrote a letter to your <u>local MP</u> to ask them to stop the closure of a local leisure centre, you might use a <u>formal register</u> (e.g. 'the closure will have a detrimental effect'). This is because the audience is an <u>authority figure</u> that you <u>don't know</u>.

If you wrote a letter to your <u>friend</u> to tell them about the leisure centre closure, you might use an <u>informal register</u> (e.g. 'it'll be rubbish when it shuts'). This is because the audience is someone you're <u>familiar</u> and <u>friendly</u> with.

4) Look out for how writers <u>adapt</u> their style and register to suit the <u>purpose</u> and the <u>audience</u> they are writing for.

My mum was always telling me to watch my tone...

Sometimes the tone of a text will jump right out at you. But watch out for texts with an ironic or sarcastic tone (see p.17) — they can be trickier. A text's style is created by lots of elements — language, structure and tone.

Words and Phrases

Writers don't just chuck in any old words — they painstakingly select them to produce the desired effect...

Words and phrases can be used to achieve different effects

1) For <u>reading</u> questions, you need to pay close attention to the reasons <u>why</u> a writer has used particular <u>words</u> or <u>phrases</u>.

Analysing the connotations of words is a way of 'reading with insight'. There's more on this on page 5.

2) Words can have subtle <u>implications</u> beyond their obvious meaning — these are called '<u>connotations</u>'. For example:

Pedro <u>shut</u> the door.

Pedro <u>slammed</u> the door.

→ When the verb 'shut' is used, it <u>doesn't</u> imply anything about Pedro's <u>emotions</u>. The verb 'slammed' has a similar meaning to 'shut', but it gives the impression that Pedro is <u>angry</u> or <u>tense</u>.

I <u>sniggered</u> when I saw Peter's costume.

I <u>chuckled</u> when I saw Peter's costume.

→ The verbs 'sniggered' and 'chuckled' both mean the writer <u>laughed</u>, but 'sniggered' has a slightly <u>nastier</u> connotation — as if the writer is making fun of Peter.

3) Words are often chosen to achieve particular <u>effects</u>. For example:

<u>my</u> dear reader

<u>your</u> beloved pet

→ Phrases that use the <u>possessive determiners</u> 'my', 'your' and 'our' help to establish <u>familiarity</u> between the writer and the reader.

Determiners are words that help to identify nouns — in this case, they show who the noun belongs to.

a <u>fundamentally</u> flawed proposition

a <u>totally</u> unbelievable situation

→ Some phrases use <u>intensifiers</u> to make the text seem more <u>emotive</u> and <u>powerful</u>. Intensifiers are adverbs like 'very', 'really' or 'extremely' that are used <u>alongside</u> strong adjectives to provide <u>emphasis</u>.

Words work together to create cumulative effects

1) Writers can use the words from a specific <u>semantic field</u> (the words associated with a particular <u>theme</u> or <u>topic</u>) to convey an idea to the reader. For example:

Dessert was simply <u>divine</u>; a <u>cloud-like</u> puff of pastry that was lighter than an <u>angel's wing</u>.

→ Here, the <u>semantic field</u> of <u>heaven</u> is used to make something sound <u>appealing</u>.

2) Keep an eye out for situations where particular <u>types</u> of words are <u>repeated</u>, e.g. sentences with lots of <u>adjectives</u> or paragraphs with lots of <u>verbs</u>.

3) You could comment on the <u>cumulative effect</u> of particular types of words — show you've thought about how the words in the text <u>work together</u> to create <u>tone</u> or <u>affect</u> the reader in some way, e.g.

Adjectives like 'electrifying', 'thrilling', 'tense' and 'intriguing' create a cumulative effect of <u>excitement</u>.

The adverbs 'jovially', 'readily' and 'pleasantly' combine to create an impression of <u>enjoyment</u>.

Relax, it's just a phrase...

It's important to identify the different types of words that a writer is using (see p.80), but you also need to analyse their effect. Think about why those words and phrases have been used and the impression they create.

Imagery

Imagery is when a writer uses language to create a vivid picture in the reader's mind.

Metaphors and similes are comparisons

1) Metaphors and similes describe one thing by comparing it to something else.

> Metaphors describe something by saying that it is something else. → *His gaze was a laser beam, shooting straight through me.*

> Similes describe something by saying that it's like something else. They usually use the words as or like. → *Walking through the bog was like wading through treacle.*

Similes made Jeremy feel as if the world had been turned upside down.

2) They help writers to make their descriptions more creative and interesting.

3) Metaphors usually create a more powerful image than similes, because they describe something as if it actually were something else.

Analogies are really fancy comparisons

1) An analogy compares one idea to another to make it easier to understand.

2) Analogies provide powerful and memorable images. They can be more familiar or more shocking than the original idea, which makes it easier for the reader to grasp the point. For example:

> *Deforestation is happening at an incredible speed. An area of rainforest equal to twenty football pitches is lost every minute.* → By comparing the area to football pitches, the writer makes it easier to visualise the scale of the problem.

Personification is describing a thing as a person

1) Personification describes something as if it's a person. This could be in the way something looks, moves, sounds or some other aspect of it. For example:

> **Describing an object as if it were alive**
> *The desk groaned under the weight of the books.*

> **Describing an abstract idea as if it were alive**
> *Fear stalked the children with every step they took.*

> **Describing an animal as if it were a person**
> *The cunning fox smiled with a self-satisfied grin.*

2) Personification makes a description more vivid (so it 'comes to life' for the reader).

3) It can also help to give a sense of the viewpoint or attitude of the writer or character:

> *Military helicopters prowled the city, their menacing mechanical voices threatening to stamp out the smallest sign of activity.* → This shows that the writer feels that the helicopters are an intimidating presence.

I think I may have developed analogy to this page...

Metaphors, similes, personification and analogies are all used to make a piece of writing more interesting. Whenever you're writing about them, make sure you concentrate on the effect they have on the reader.

Language Features

Writers use lots of techniques to engage their reader and emphasise their points — here are four more...

Alliteration and onomatopoeia are about how words sound

1) Alliteration and onomatopoeia use the <u>sounds</u> of words to create an <u>effect</u>:

<u>Alliteration</u> is when words that are close together begin with the <u>same sound</u>. →	*PM's panic!* *Fairytale finish for Fred* *Close call for kids* *Mum's magic medicine*

<u>Onomatopoeic</u> words <u>sound</u> <u>like</u> the noises they describe. →	*thud* *crackle* *gulp* *squish* *whistle* *hiss* *smash* *boom*

2) <u>Alliteration</u> helps a writer to grab a reader's <u>attention</u>. It's often used for <u>emphasis</u> and to make key points more <u>memorable</u>.

3) <u>Onomatopoeia</u> makes descriptions more <u>powerful</u> — it appeals to the reader's sense of <u>hearing</u>, which helps them <u>imagine</u> what the writer is describing.

Oxymorons are phrases that appear to contradict each other

1) An oxymoron is a phrase that <u>makes sense</u> but seems to <u>contradict itself</u>, because the words have <u>meanings</u> that don't seem to <u>fit together</u>.

2) Writers will sometimes use an oxymoron to <u>draw attention</u> to a particular <u>idea</u>.

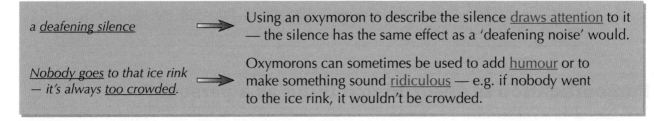

a <u>*deafening silence*</u> →	Using an oxymoron to describe the silence <u>draws attention</u> to it — the silence has the same effect as a 'deafening noise' would.
<u>*Nobody goes*</u> *to that ice rink — it's always <u>too crowded</u>.* →	Oxymorons can sometimes be used to add <u>humour</u> or to make something sound <u>ridiculous</u> — e.g. if nobody went to the ice rink, it wouldn't be crowded.

Hyperbole is intentional exaggeration

1) <u>Hyperbole</u> is where a writer <u>deliberately exaggerates</u> something.

2) It can be a very <u>powerful</u> way of making a point.

Hyperbole is an example of a rhetorical device — see p.18.

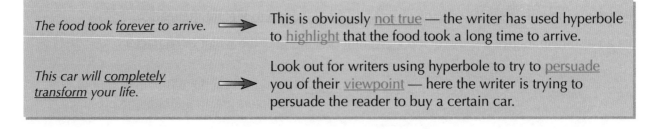

The food took <u>forever</u> to arrive. →	This is obviously <u>not true</u> — the writer has used hyperbole to <u>highlight</u> that the food took a long time to arrive.
This car will <u>completely</u> <u>transform</u> your life. →	Look out for writers using hyperbole to try to <u>persuade</u> you of their <u>viewpoint</u> — here the writer is trying to persuade the reader to buy a certain car.

Hyperbole — the greatest literary technique known to man...

Challenge #1 is learning to spell 'onomatopoeia'... But once you've got your head around that, you can enjoy the best bloomin' page I've ever made. Or maybe it's the worst — these oxymorons have got to me...

Section Three — English Language: Style and Techniques

Irony and Sarcasm

Irony and sarcasm are two more techniques to watch out for. They're pretty similar, but irony is a bit friendlier.

Irony is saying the opposite of what you mean

1) Irony is when the <u>literal meaning</u> of a piece of writing is the exact <u>opposite</u> of its <u>intended meaning</u>.

2) The reader can tell the writer is being ironic from the <u>context</u> of the writing.

3) Writers often use irony to express their viewpoint, but it helps to make what they're saying more <u>humorous</u> or <u>light-hearted</u>.

> *It was pouring down with rain — perfect weather for a barbecue.* → The <u>context</u> (the rainy weather) shows that the writer actually means that it was <u>terrible</u> weather for a barbecue.

> *Yet again I was off to see my favourite person — the dentist.* → The phrase "<u>Yet again</u>" hints that this isn't something the writer wants to do. The dentist <u>isn't</u> actually the writer's favourite person — they're being <u>ironic</u>.

Sarcasm is nastier than irony

1) <u>Sarcasm</u> is language that has a <u>mocking</u> or <u>scornful</u> tone. It's often intended to <u>insult someone</u> or <u>make fun</u> of them, or to show that the writer is <u>angry</u> or <u>annoyed</u> about something.

2) Sarcastic writing usually uses <u>irony</u> — but the tone is more <u>aggressive</u> and <u>unpleasant</u>.

Phil couldn't believe how many people liked his new hat.

> *The food took 90 minutes to arrive, which was just brilliant. I can think of no better way to spend a Saturday evening than waiting around for a plate of mediocre mush.* → The writer's used <u>irony</u> and a <u>sarcastic</u> tone to show his <u>frustration</u> and <u>anger</u> — it's meant to <u>insult</u> the restaurant that kept him waiting.

Satire is used to mock people or society

1) <u>Satire</u> is a kind of writing that uses irony and sarcasm to <u>make fun</u> of a particular person or thing. It makes a <u>comment</u> on the <u>shortcomings</u> or <u>stupidity</u> of that person or aspect of society.

2) It's used particularly in <u>journalism</u> or <u>reviews</u>, and is often directed at politicians or topical issues.

> *Travelling by train has become a test of how well you can imitate a tinned sardine. If cramming people into a carriage was an Olympic sport, us Brits would be guaranteed a gold medal.* → The writer uses <u>satire</u> to criticise the experience of travelling by train. Satirical writers usually hope that <u>pointing out</u> a <u>fault</u> in society may lead to the fault being <u>corrected</u> or <u>improved</u>.

This page is great — I just love sarcasm...

If the writer is being surprisingly positive or negative about something, then that's a good clue that irony or sarcasm might be at work. It should be fairly clear when they're being used — otherwise they'd be pointless.

Rhetoric and Bias

Rhetorical techniques make language more persuasive — they try to influence the reader in a certain way. If a text is biased, it doesn't give a balanced view — the writer's opinion affects the writing and its message.

There are lots of rhetorical techniques

Think about how other techniques (e.g. alliteration, sarcasm and hyperbole) could also be used as rhetorical devices.

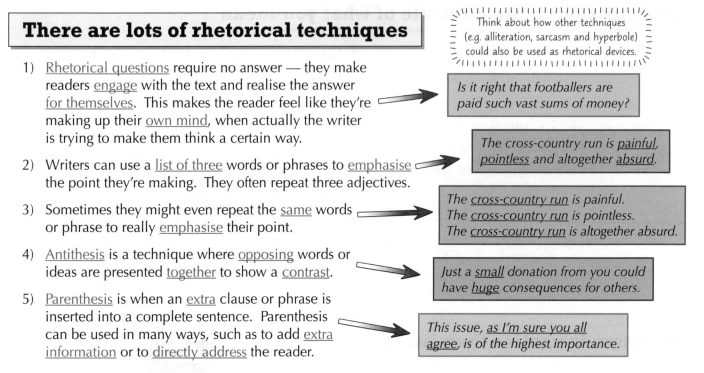

1) <u>Rhetorical questions</u> require no answer — they make readers <u>engage</u> with the text and realise the answer <u>for themselves</u>. This makes the reader feel like they're making up their <u>own mind</u>, when actually the writer is trying to make them think a certain way.

Is it right that footballers are paid such vast sums of money?

2) Writers can use a <u>list of three</u> words or phrases to <u>emphasise</u> the point they're making. They often repeat three adjectives.

The cross-country run is <u>painful</u>, <u>pointless</u> and altogether <u>absurd</u>.

3) Sometimes they might even repeat the <u>same</u> words or phrase to really <u>emphasise</u> their point.

The <u>cross-country run</u> is painful.
The <u>cross-country run</u> is pointless.
The <u>cross-country run</u> is altogether absurd.

4) <u>Antithesis</u> is a technique where <u>opposing</u> words or ideas are presented <u>together</u> to show a <u>contrast</u>.

Just a <u>small</u> donation from you could have <u>huge</u> consequences for others.

5) <u>Parenthesis</u> is when an <u>extra</u> clause or phrase is inserted into a complete sentence. Parenthesis can be used in many ways, such as to add <u>extra</u> <u>information</u> or to <u>directly address</u> the reader.

This issue, <u>as I'm sure you all agree</u>, is of the highest importance.

Biased writing is affected by the writer's opinions

1) Biased writers don't usually lie, but they don't give the <u>full picture</u>.

2) Sometimes the writer <u>won't mention</u> something that opposes their viewpoint, or they'll <u>exaggerate</u> something that supports it.

3) Biased writing also often uses <u>generalisations</u> — sweeping statements that don't apply in all situations.

4) Bias isn't always <u>obvious</u>, or even <u>deliberate</u>. Biased writers often <u>seem</u> to be talking in a neutral, factual way — while actually only presenting one point of view.

5) You need to be able to <u>recognise</u> bias, so that you don't mistake opinion for fact.

6) Look out for bias in non-fiction texts like <u>newspaper articles</u>, <u>autobiographies</u> and <u>reviews</u>.

Sylvester's essay on who was boss wasn't the slightest bit biased.

Aigburth United were desperately unlucky not to win on Saturday night. They defended like heroes throughout the match, and only a shocking refereeing decision prevented a glorious victory.

Watch out for <u>emotive language</u>, e.g. "heroes", and statements that could be <u>opinions</u>, e.g. "desperately unlucky" and "shocking refereeing decision". They will help you work out if a text is <u>biased</u> or not.

Revision is a fun, exciting, thrilling way to spend a Friday night...

Rhetoric is a powerful tool, but I'm not sure it can convince us to love revision... If you see lots of rhetoric in a text, then there's a good chance that it might be biased — these two techniques often hang out together.

Narrative Viewpoint and Descriptive Language

All literary texts have a narrator — a voice that's telling the story. Literary writers love to use descriptive language — words that create pictures in the reader's mind.

The narrative viewpoint is usually quite easy to spot

1) A first-person narrator tells the story using words like 'I', 'we' and 'me'. A first-person narrator is often one of the characters, telling the reader directly about their feelings and experiences.

> *I stood in the wings of the stage, waiting my turn, fear coursing through my veins.* → A first-person narrator establishes a stronger, more personal connection with the reader.

2) A second-person narrator tells the story using words like 'you'. A second-person narrator talks as if the reader ('you') is one of the characters.

> *You turn your head to see her walking towards you. Your heart begins to race.* → A second-person narrator makes the reader 'feel' what the character is feeling.

3) A third-person narrator is not one of the characters. They tell the story using words like 'he' and 'she' to talk about the characters.

> *Ian's elated expression could mean only one thing: he had got a place at medical school.* → A third-person narrator has a more detached viewpoint.

> Some third-person narrators are omniscient — they know what all the characters are thinking. Others are limited — they only know what one character is thinking.

4) When writing about a narrator, think about how reliable they are. You might not be able to trust them fully if they don't know something, or if they're trying to affect the reader in some way.

Descriptive language makes text interesting

1) Writers use descriptive techniques and vocabulary so that the reader gets a really clear image in their mind of what the writer's describing. It makes the text more interesting, dramatic and convincing.

2) Descriptive techniques include imagery such as metaphors, similes and personification (see p.15).

3) Writers often give descriptions based on their five senses (what they can see, smell, hear, touch or taste).

4) Another sign of descriptive language is when the writer uses lots of adjectives — describing words like 'huge' or 'fiery' that give a specific impression of something.

5) Writers might also use interesting verbs, such as 'saunter' instead of 'walk' to make their descriptions really specific.

> *The sun was setting over the sea. The view from the beach was incredible.* → This example relies on the reader to picture for themselves what a nice sunset might look like.

> *The salty sea air whooshed around me as the dark orange sun melted into the horizon, dyeing the cobalt sky a deep crimson.* → This one uses interesting adjectives and verbs to help the reader to picture and even 'feel' what's going on.

6) Writers can also build up the description of something throughout their work. For example, by writing sentences with contrasting descriptions or descriptions that agree with each other.

My dad used descriptive language when I scratched his car...

Descriptive language comes in all shapes and sizes — look out for it in texts and write about the effect it has. It's easy to forget about the narrator, but try to think about how they speak and whether you can trust them.

Structure

Structure is all about the order in which writers present events and ideas to the reader.

Structure is important for fiction and non-fiction

1) <u>Structure</u> is the way a writer <u>organises</u> their <u>ideas</u> within a text.

2) In <u>non-fiction</u> texts, writers will use structure to help them achieve their <u>purpose</u>. This might be to:

- Build their <u>argument</u> to a powerful conclusion.
- Reinforce the <u>persuasive</u> elements of their text through repetition.
- Set out an <u>informative</u> text in a clear and balanced way.
- Order their <u>advice</u> in a logical and easy-to-follow way.

3) In <u>fiction</u> texts, writers will structure their work in a way they think will <u>entertain</u> the reader. For example, story writing could have a <u>linear</u> or <u>non-linear</u> structure:

Texts with a <u>linear</u> structure are arranged <u>chronologically</u> — events are described in the order in which they happened and the text <u>flows</u> naturally from <u>beginning</u> to <u>middle</u> to <u>end</u>.

Texts with a <u>non-linear</u> structure are ordered in a way that makes the text <u>interesting</u>, rather than in chronological order. They might include things like <u>flashbacks</u>, changes in <u>perspective</u> or <u>time shifts</u>.

4) Linear texts tend to <u>build</u> towards some form of <u>climax</u>, whilst non-linear texts might <u>begin</u> with a <u>dramatic moment</u> and work <u>backwards</u> from there.

5) Whenever you write about <u>structure</u>, you need to show <u>how</u> the writer has used structure to produce a particular <u>effect</u> on the reader.

Writers use structure to focus the reader's attention

1) One of the easiest ways to write about <u>structure</u> is to think about how the writer is <u>directing</u> your <u>attention</u> as you read. There are lots of ways a writer can do this, for example:

- The writer might draw the reader in by <u>describing</u> something <u>general</u>, then <u>narrow</u> their <u>focus</u> down to something more <u>specific</u>.
- The writer could <u>describe</u> things along a <u>journey</u> and make you feel as if you are travelling with them. This might involve moving from the <u>outside</u> to the <u>inside</u> or just from one place to another.
- A text might start with <u>description</u> and then move on to <u>dialogue</u>. This would shift your focus from <u>setting</u> to <u>characters</u>.
- Often, a writer will use a <u>new paragraph</u> to start a <u>new topic</u>. This could be a <u>smooth</u> transition or it could have a <u>jarring</u> effect that draws the reader's attention to a particular part of the text.
- In <u>non-fiction</u> texts, the writer will usually use paragraphs to <u>lead</u> you from their <u>introduction</u>, through their <u>main points</u> and onto their <u>conclusion</u>.

2) Often, <u>descriptive</u> writing will <u>show</u> rather than <u>tell</u> the reader what to <u>focus</u> on. For example, it might move the reader's attention from one place to another, acting like a camera shot does in a film. This type of writing is often called <u>cinematic writing</u>.

Structure

The narrative viewpoint will affect the structure

1) The <u>narrator</u> controls what the reader <u>sees</u> and what <u>information</u> they <u>receive</u>.

2) The narrator might <u>withhold</u> some information to create <u>tension</u>, or they could <u>skip</u> over certain parts of a story because they are <u>biased</u>.

3) Different <u>narrators</u> will have different <u>effects</u> on the <u>structure</u> of a text:

"When you're a grown-up narrator, you can skip about too."

- A <u>third-person</u> narrator (see page 19) will often have an <u>overall</u> view of the story, and so the structure might <u>skip around</u> to cover lots of <u>different</u> events.

- For texts with a <u>first-person</u> narrator, the structure will probably <u>follow</u> that character's experiences quite <u>closely</u>.

4) Look out for texts that have <u>more than one</u> narrator. This might mean that the structure <u>jumps around</u> or alternates between the different <u>perspectives</u>.

5) Some texts use a <u>frame</u> narrative — this is when one story is presented <u>within</u> another. For example, the writer might use one character to <u>narrate</u> a story to <u>another</u> character. This allows the writer to move between <u>multiple settings</u> and sets of <u>characters</u>.

Writers use different sentence forms to interest the reader

1) Varying the <u>length</u> of sentences can create different <u>effects</u>. Here are a couple of <u>examples</u>:

The sky was growing darker. I couldn't see where I was going. I stumbled. ⟹	Short simple sentences can be used to <u>build tension</u> or to create a <u>worried</u> and <u>confused</u> tone.

These are just examples — the effects of different sentence lengths will vary from text to text.

I waited excitedly at the foot of the stairs, listening to the footsteps above, thinking about the afternoon ahead, pacing the hall and counting down the minutes until we could set off. ⟹	A longer, complex sentence could be used to give the impression of <u>time dragging</u>.

2) The <u>order</u> of words within sentences can also be chosen to create an <u>effect</u>. For example:

I had <u>never</u> seen such chaos <u>before</u>. *<u>Never before</u> had I seen such chaos.* ⟹	Writers sometimes use <u>inversion</u> (<u>altering</u> the normal word order) to change the <u>emphasis</u> in a text. Here, inversion helps to emphasise the phrase '<u>Never before</u>'.

3) If you notice something about the way a writer has used sentences, don't just identify it — you need to <u>analyse</u> the <u>effects</u> to show how they <u>influence</u> the reader.

Life without structure would be pretty flat...

Structure is really important to literary texts — without it, the reader may well miss the writer's intentions or message. You need to think about how the writer is using structure to direct your attention to certain things.

Writing with Purpose

All writing has a purpose — even this introduction, which is here to explain that this page is about purpose.

Structure your writing to suit your purpose

See pages 9-11 for more about writer's purpose.

1) The purpose of your writing might be to <u>inform</u>, <u>advise</u>, <u>argue</u> or <u>persuade</u>, or <u>entertain</u>. It could even be <u>more than one</u> of these.

2) Sometimes it will be <u>obvious</u> what the <u>purpose</u> of your writing needs to be, e.g. you might be asked to write a letter to argue or persuade. It can be <u>less obvious</u> though, so sometimes you'll need to <u>work it out</u>, e.g. if you're asked to write a story, your purpose would be to entertain.

3) Different purposes will need different <u>structures</u>, so you'll need to think about a <u>structure</u> that will help you achieve your purpose most effectively.

4) You can lay out your structure by writing a <u>plan</u>, so that it stays <u>consistent</u> throughout your answer:

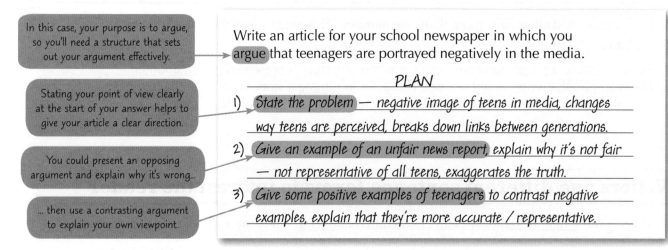

In this case, your purpose is to argue, so you'll need a structure that sets out your argument effectively.

Stating your point of view clearly at the start of your answer helps to give your article a clear direction.

You could present an opposing argument and explain why it's wrong...

... then use a contrasting argument to explain your own viewpoint.

Write an article for your school newspaper in which you argue that teenagers are portrayed negatively in the media.

PLAN

1) *State the problem — negative image of teens in media, changes way teens are perceived, breaks down links between generations.*

2) *Give an example of an unfair news report, explain why it's not fair — not representative of all teens, exaggerates the truth.*

3) *Give some positive examples of teenagers to contrast negative examples, explain that they're more accurate / representative.*

Choose your tone, style and register to match your purpose

1) You need to show that you can <u>adjust</u> your <u>tone</u>, <u>style</u> and <u>register</u> (see p.13) to suit your purpose.

2) For example, an <u>informative</u> text might have a <u>serious</u>, <u>reserved</u> style, with a <u>formal</u> register:

The UK's younger generation show signs of frustration at the way they are perceived. Studies show that up to 95% of 18-24 year-olds feel that their stance on environmentalism is being ignored.

This text uses <u>technical terms</u>, <u>facts</u> and <u>statistics</u> to help clearly inform the reader.

3) A <u>persuasive</u> text needs to be more <u>subjective</u> (based on personal feelings). It might try to create a <u>personal</u> tone that involves the reader in a text:

See p.18 for some rhetorical techniques that help to achieve this.

Like me, you must be weary of the incessant criticism. We're intelligent young citizens who understand the issues threatening our planet. Why are we being ignored?

This text uses a <u>rhetorical question</u> and the pronouns 'you' and 'we' to <u>involve</u> and <u>persuade</u> its audience.

4) When you adjust your <u>writing</u> to suit your purpose, make sure you still use <u>sophisticated vocabulary</u>.

This revision guide's purpose is to get you through your exams...

Don't forget that writing can often have more than one purpose — make sure you think about all the reasons that you're writing, so that you can adapt your style and produce a top-quality piece of writing. Easy peasy.

Writing for an Audience

For each writing task, you'll need to bear in mind your audience. Your audience is just anyone who's going to hear or read your writing — it doesn't mean you'll have to perform your work to a room full of strangers...

Work out who your audience is

1) Usually the question will specify a particular audience:

> You are going to submit a short story to a magazine.
> The magazine is aimed at young people aged 14-18.
>
> Write a short story about somebody who has travelled a long way.

Here's the audience — 'young people aged 14-18'.

2) Sometimes you might need to work out from the question who your audience is. The form and content will give you some clues:

This statement is about schools, so the audience will be people interested in education, such as parents or teachers.

> 'Students should attend classes virtually. In today's digital society, it's illogical that students still have to leave the house to go to school.'

You're writing a broadsheet newspaper article, so your audience will mostly be well-educated adults.

> Write a broadsheet newspaper article in which you explain your point of view on this statement.

Choose your tone, style and register to match your audience

1) You'll need to adapt your tone, style and register so that it suits your audience.

2) For example, you might want to consider the age and level of expertise of your audience, as well as your relationship with them.

See p.13 for more on tone, style and register.

Age

- If you're addressing a younger audience, you might use a more light-hearted tone and an informal register, with a colloquial or chatty style.

- A formal, serious register that doesn't use any slang might work better for older audiences. You might also use a more complex style than you would for a younger audience.

Expertise

- Different audiences will have different levels of expertise in the subject you're writing about.

- For example, if you're writing a report for a panel of experts, your register should be more formal, with a style that uses more specialised language than if you were writing for a general audience.

Relationship with reader

- If you're writing to a familiar audience, like a friend, you might write in an informal register, and use a friendly tone.

- If you're writing to an unknown audience, it would be better to use an impersonal tone and a formal register.

3) You should always aim to show your writing skills to the examiner — even if you're writing informally or for a young audience, you still need to make sure you include a range of vocabulary and sentence types.

I don't believe it, she's written an essay! And the crowd goes wild!

You'll be pleased to hear that your audience won't actually be there in the exam room — although I suppose it might be nice to have a group of people to applaud you whenever you craft a particularly good sentence...

Writing Stories

Story-writing is a task that might pop up. You might have to write a short story, or focus on writing a particular bit, like the opening or the ending. It's time to sharpen up those storytelling skills...

Grab your reader's attention from the start

1) It's always a good idea to <u>start</u> your stories with an <u>opening sentence</u> that'll make your <u>reader</u> want to <u>carry on</u> reading. For example:

   You could start with a <u>direct address</u> to the reader:

   > *Everybody has a bad day now and again, don't they? Well, I'm going to tell you about a day that was much, much worse than your worst day ever.*

   Or you could try a description of a particularly <u>unusual character</u>:

   > *Humphrey Ward was, without a shadow of a doubt, the most brilliant (and most cantankerous) banana thief in the country.*

Grabbing attention had never been a problem for Marvin.

Try to avoid clichéd openings like 'Once upon a time'.

2) If you start your story in the <u>middle of the action</u>, it'll create a <u>fast-paced</u> atmosphere that makes the reader want to find out <u>what happens next</u>:

   > *I couldn't believe it. He was gone. "He must be here," I thought to myself as I went through the shed, desperately throwing aside box after box. It was no use. Peter had run away, and it was all my fault.*

3) This example <u>explains</u> some of what's happening after a few sentences, which keeps up the <u>fast pace</u> of the narrative — so the story stays <u>interesting</u>.

4) You could also try <u>prolonging</u> the mystery to create <u>tension</u> in your narrative. Just make sure you <u>reveal</u> what's going on before it gets too <u>confusing</u> for your audience.

5) However you start your writing, you need to make sure it's <u>engaging</u> and <u>entertaining</u> for the reader — so whatever you do, don't <u>waffle</u>.

Try to build the tension from the start

Your school is making a creative writing anthology that will be sold to other pupils. You have decided to submit a piece of writing.

Write the opening part of a story about a trip to the beach.

> The waves drowned out my shouts as they crashed against the rocks with thundering force. I had only closed my eyes for a minute, and now I had awoken to find that Amy was nowhere to be seen. I scanned the deserted beach, searching for any sign of my beautiful daughter.
>
> Amy had been wearing a blue pinafore dress that made her look like Alice in Wonderland. I remembered joking with her about how funny it would be if the Queen of Hearts had suddenly appeared to chase her along the sands. She had merely giggled and returned to the digging project that was taking up all her attention. But where was she now?

This story starts in the middle of the action — we don't know who the narrator is or why they're shouting.

This text solves the mystery of what's going on fairly quickly to maintain the pace.

Use key words to show as clearly as possible that you're answering the question.

Try to keep the tension building as you move on from your opening paragraphs.

Writing Stories

Make your language and narrative viewpoint fit the task

1) Different <u>word choices</u> will have different <u>effects</u>, so you'll need to pick vocabulary that creates the right <u>tone</u> for your story. For example:

> *The door screeched open and I carefully entered the dingy cellar. Shadows cast by my torch leapt up at me through the gloom.*

⟹ Words like '<u>screeched</u>', '<u>dingy</u>' and '<u>gloom</u>' make this writing sound <u>spooky</u>.

> *I burst noisily through the thicket of trees and sprinted towards the shore. The men were still chasing me, bellowing threats.*

⟹ Words like '<u>burst</u>', '<u>sprinted</u>' and '<u>chasing</u>' make this writing sound <u>exciting</u> and <u>dramatic</u>.

2) You also need to think about what <u>narrative viewpoint</u> you're going to use (see p.19).

3) A <u>first-person narrator</u> uses the pronouns 'I' and 'we', as they're usually one of the <u>characters</u> in the story.

> *I quickly scanned the book for anything that might help. My heart was racing; I knew I needed to work fast.*

⟹ The first-person narrative makes things more <u>dramatic</u> by helping the reader to <u>imagine</u> the story is happening to them.

4) A <u>third-person narrator</u> uses words like 'he' and 'she' to talk <u>about</u> the characters from a <u>separate</u> viewpoint.

> *Shamil lit the bonfire carefully, then retreated back a few metres as the feeble fire began to crackle and spit.*

⟹ The narrator isn't part of the story. This creates <u>distance</u>, as the narrative voice and the characters are <u>separate</u> from each other.

Use descriptive techniques to make your text engaging

Write the opening part of a story suggested by this picture:

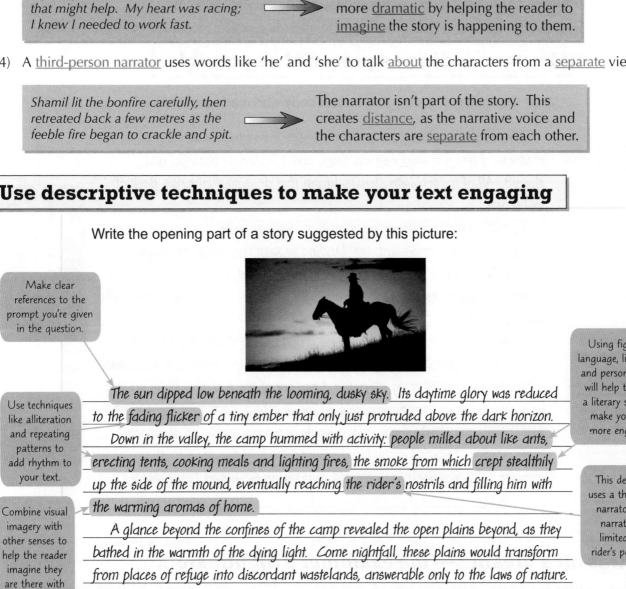

Make clear references to the prompt you're given in the question.

Use techniques like alliteration and repeating patterns to add rhythm to your text.

Combine visual imagery with other senses to help the reader imagine they are there with the narrator.

Using figurative language, like similes and personification, will help to create a literary style and make your text more engaging.

This description uses a third-person narrator, so the narrative isn't limited by the rider's perspective.

> *The sun dipped low beneath the looming, dusky sky. Its daytime glory was reduced to the fading flicker of a tiny ember that only just protruded above the dark horizon. Down in the valley, the camp hummed with activity: people milled about like ants, erecting tents, cooking meals and lighting fires, the smoke from which crept stealthily up the side of the mound, eventually reaching the rider's nostrils and filling him with the warming aromas of home.*
> *A glance beyond the confines of the camp revealed the open plains beyond, as they bathed in the warmth of the dying light. Come nightfall, these plains would transform from places of refuge into discordant wastelands, answerable only to the laws of nature.*

Writing Stories

It's important to write a good ending

1) Whether you're asked to write the <u>end</u> of a story, or a <u>different part</u>, it's still important that you <u>finish well</u> — you want to leave the examiner with a <u>great impression</u> of your writing abilities.

2) Here are some <u>examples</u> of different ways that you could <u>end</u> a story:

- You could finish with an unexpected <u>plot twist</u> that will <u>shock</u> the reader.

- You could show the <u>main character</u> coming to some kind of <u>realisation</u>.

- You could create a <u>cliffhanger</u> ending by finishing with a <u>question</u>. This will leave the reader thinking about what will happen <u>next</u>.

- You could have a <u>neat</u>, <u>happy ending</u> that will <u>satisfy</u> the reader.

Buster had come to the realisation that he was going to need a haircut.

3) If you find you're running out of time, think up a <u>quick ending</u> — make sure you show how the story ends, and finish with a short, <u>punchy</u> line.

4) Under absolutely no circumstances use the ending, "And it was all a <u>dream</u>."

Try to make your ending as powerful as possible

Write the ending of a story about somebody who made a bad decision.

The narrator has had a realisation, which hints to the reader that the story is about to come to an end.

I knew I should never have stolen the vase. It had been a moment of madness. I had just seen it sitting there, and it looked so beautiful and elegant. All of my problems stemmed from that decision, that single flash of foolishness.

I spent a long time wondering what to do with the vase. I studied it intently. It was too beautiful to discard, too dazzling to keep concealed any longer. Eventually, I made a decision. I took it to the cliff and threw it over, watching it smash on the rocks below. It was an awful sight, but at least my guilty secret was gone forever.

Your final paragraphs should build the tension towards a climax that will resolve the action.

After you've given a satisfying ending, you could go on to add an unexpected twist that leaves the reader with doubt in their mind.

Late that night, the wind was howling around my tent, and the rain was pelting down on the canvas. Suddenly, there was a huge crash of thunder and a blinding flash of lightning. Terrified, I ran out of the tent, only to be greeted by a strange apparition: there, sitting on top of a tree stump, was the missing vase. It was completely whole. Not a single crack was visible on its smooth, shiny exterior. I whirled around and scoured the field for any sign of an intruder. That was when I saw the old, hunched man walking slowly away.

However you end your text, make sure it's exciting and powerful.

"It was all a dream" — the examiner's nightmare...

Seriously — steer as far away as you can from clichéd endings. All they do is prove to the examiner that you haven't thought very hard about your answer, as well as making your story more boring than double Physics.

Writing Descriptions

You could be asked to write a description of a character or scene. The aim is to give your audience a detailed idea of what you're describing, so you'll need to use words to paint a vivid, interesting picture in their mind.

Descriptions are detailed

1) Descriptions use strong <u>visual</u> language to create an <u>impression</u> of a person or place for the reader.

2) You <u>don't</u> need to include as much <u>plot</u> or <u>action</u> — focus mostly on <u>describing</u> the subject.

3) Even though there's no <u>plot</u>, you still need to have some <u>structure</u> to your writing — e.g. you could start with a <u>general</u> description, then go on to describe some more <u>specific</u> details.

4) The purpose of a description is normally to <u>entertain</u> the reader, so you need to adapt your writing <u>style</u> accordingly, and keep your <u>language</u> interesting.

5) Descriptions need <u>detail</u>. For example, a <u>character</u> description might include:

- A character's <u>physical features</u>, e.g. hair colour, clothing.

- A character's <u>personality</u>, e.g. they could be funny, serious, reserved, extroverted.

- Any other particular <u>features</u> that reveal <u>more</u> about them, e.g. any nervous habits.

- Your <u>personal opinion</u>, e.g. what you like or dislike about them.

Alice had nearly forgotten to describe Maria's habit.

Use language to describe a character or scene

Write a character description about someone who is intimidating.

You can use the character's habits to create an impression of their personality.

The woman's fingernails tapped impatiently against the wood of the mantelpiece. She was standing still, but the motion of her perfectly-manicured fingernails, and the impatient huffs of air that were regularly expelled from between her thin lips, made her seem restless and agitated. Somehow she gave off the impression that she never really stopped moving.

One way to structure your writing is to start with a tiny detail, then expand outwards.

Use figurative language to show off your descriptive skills.

She was an angular exclamation mark of a woman, and she stuck out like a sore thumb against our familiar, homely surroundings. She wore her dark hair short; it had been meticulously combed into an unforgiving style that cut into her sharp cheekbones. Her suit was an inky black colour, which only served to emphasise her militantly slender form. When she spoke, her voice was low and commanding, and her expression was set into a permanent frown that was half-angry, half-distracted, and wholly intimidating.

She was the most terrifying person I had ever met.

Use the five senses to create a really detailed description.

You can write from any narrative viewpoint, as long as it's appropriate to your purpose and audience.

Don't lose your focus — remember that your answer needs to be about somebody intimidating.

How do you contact the Ancient Egyptians? Write to de scribe...

You can really pull out all the weapons in your descriptive arsenal for this one — go to town with metaphors, similes, alliteration, personification, adjectives, the five senses, repetition, onomatopoeia, hyperbole — and lists...

Writing Newspaper Articles

Read all about it... students might be asked to write a newspaper article... read all about it.

Newspaper articles report events and offer opinions

1) A newspaper's main purpose is to <u>inform</u> people about <u>current affairs</u> and <u>other topics</u> that people are interested in.

2) They do this in <u>two main ways</u>:

By directly reporting news

- Some newspaper articles are written to convey <u>facts</u> about a <u>story</u> or <u>theme</u>.

- They may report the viewpoints of <u>other people</u>, but the writer will not directly express their <u>own viewpoint</u> on a subject.

- The writer's <u>own viewpoint</u> might come across through the viewpoints of the people they <u>choose to quote</u>.

By writing commentaries

- Commentaries (also called <u>columns</u> or <u>opinion pieces</u>) offer the <u>viewpoint</u> of the <u>writer</u> on a news story or an important theme.

- Commentaries <u>entertain</u> their audience, as readers engage with the <u>personality</u> of the writer by <u>agreeing</u> or <u>disagreeing</u> with their opinions and insights.

Newspaper articles need to engage their audience

1) <u>News reports</u> are trying to convey facts, so they'll use an <u>unemotional tone</u>.

2) The register may be <u>technical</u> and the style quite <u>sophisticated</u>, in order to make the information seem <u>accurate</u> and <u>reliable</u>.

The author of the controversial report, Professor Mannings, has stated that, "agricultural reform is necessary to build a sustainable future". The report has, however, attracted widespread criticism from members of the agricultural community.	This conveys information in a <u>direct</u> way, using an <u>impersonal</u> tone, and with sophisticated, precise vocabulary. Viewpoints are conveyed by <u>quoting</u> and <u>paraphrasing</u>.

3) <u>Opinion pieces</u> often use a <u>personal</u> tone, a more <u>informal</u> register and a <u>conversational</u> style to help convey the opinions and personality of the writer.

It seems to me that this lot all need to take a deep breath and stop whinging. Nobody's going to bulldoze our green spaces any time soon — they'll have to spend 25 years making a planning application first.	This uses <u>colloquial</u> words to create a conversational tone and <u>sarcasm</u> to convey the viewpoint of the writer.

4) <u>Rhetorical techniques</u> (see p.18) are commonly used in commentaries to help get the writer's opinions across forcefully and to encourage readers to <u>agree</u> with the writer.

What happened to the good old days, when the presence of a heap of spuds on the table at dinnertime brought delight all round? Has all this 'health food' nonsense made us forget our faithful starchy friend?	This uses <u>rhetorical questions</u> to engage and persuade the reader.

Writing Newspaper Articles

Newspapers have varying audiences

1) Newspapers are broadly split into two types — tabloids and broadsheets.

2) Tabloids (such as *The Sun* and *The Mirror*) tend to focus on more sensational topics and people, making their news stories accessible and with a wide appeal.

3) Broadsheets (such as *The Telegraph* and *The Guardian*) are thought of as more formal, 'high-brow' journalism — focusing on what are thought to be more sophisticated topics.

4) In the exam, you might be told what form to write in, e.g. 'a broadsheet newspaper article' — make sure you adapt your tone, style and register to the right audience.

5) Most newspapers also publish articles on the Internet. If you're asked to write a news article for an online audience, think about how your audience might be different (e.g. younger or with a different level of understanding about the subject), and adapt your writing to suit.

Make sure your article gives your opinion

A well-known travel writer has published an article in which she claims that guided tours are 'uncultured', and that the only way to see the 'true heart of a country' is by going 'off the beaten track'.

You have been asked to write an article for a broadsheet newspaper in which you explain your opinion on the travel writer's comments.

This question is asking you to give your opinion on a topic.

Make sure you link your answer to the prompts you're given in the question.

Opinion articles often combine a relatively informal style with complex sentences and vocabulary.

You're giving an opinion, so your tone should be quite personal.

Use rhetorical devices like repetition to make your writing entertaining and persuasive.

You can use a sarcastic tone to give your writing a sense of personality.

At some point or other, we've all been faced with a travel snob: that particular breed of rough-and-tumble traveller who knows all about where to go, what to see and, most importantly, how to see it. The travel snob thinks that guided tours are for the 'uncultured' bores of this planet. The travel snob believes in travel without a destination. And yet, the travel snob will always find time to tell you about a 'hidden gem' that only they can take you to.

You would think someone so educated in the ways of the world would have realised the irony by now — travel snobs are themselves tour guides. The places that they think are 'off the beaten track' are transported, by their own recommendation, right onto 'the beaten track'. They are the one beating the track; they are leading the tourists away from their well-populated honeypot attractions into 'the heart of things'.

In the meantime, guided tours are often run by local people, who will frequently have a real treasure trove of local knowledge. How can a throwaway recommendation from an outsider possibly surpass that? Anybody who wants to see the 'true heart of a country' must be guided by the people who live in it.

"Why do you prefer broad sheets?" "I've got a really wide bed..."

It's worth having a look at some real newspaper articles as part of your revision. You'll soon start to spot some patterns in the vocabulary and structure that they use, which you can use to help you write a top-notch answer.

Biographical Writing and Diary Entries

Biographies and diaries are both types of writing that are used for recording what happens in people's lives.

Biographical writing and diary entries are similar

Biographical writing and diary entries are texts that focus on recounting events and feelings.

Diary entries

- Diary entries are private and personal — the writer is writing to themselves.

- You should write in the first person and try to include a sense of personality in your writing. To achieve this, you could use an informal register with colloquial language or humour.

- The tone of a diary entry can vary depending on what you're writing about — you'll need to adapt your tone so that it's appropriate to the events and emotions you're trying to convey.

Biographies and autobiographies

- There are two types of biographical writing — autobiographies, in which the writer is writing about their own life, and biographies, in which the writer is writing about somebody else's life.

- Autobiographies are written in the first person. Biographies are written in the third person, although they focus on the perspective and feelings of the person they're about.

- Biographical writing is usually written with quite a formal register, as it's normally written for a wide audience. However it can sometimes be less formal, particularly in autobiographies, where the writer is trying to convey a sense of their personality to the audience.

Diaries have a personal tone

Write a diary entry in which you explain your point of view on the idea of keeping animals as pets.

Thursday 22nd January

Mother said today that she doesn't like the way we keep our dog, or even us having a pet dog at all. She thinks it's cruel to keep animals in captivity. I don't think you can really call our house 'captivity' (even if it does feel like that sometimes) but I suppose it is a bit selfish. We moved Curly into an unfamiliar environment without a second thought.

Mother also says that we shouldn't keep pets cooped up in houses, as they should be running around freely outdoors. I disagree: I don't think it's wrong that we keep pets indoors most of the time, as long as they're happy. I do think it's important that owners focus on the wellbeing of their pets, but I don't think that necessarily means forcing them to live outdoors.

Starting off with a counter-argument can help you to express your viewpoint.

The question has asked for your point of view, so make sure that you're expressing your opinions clearly.

The tone of your diary entry should be relaxed, so it's fine to include humour and colloquial phrases.

Even though a diary is informal, try to use a good range of sentence structures.

Dear Diary, today I learnt lots of exciting stuff about biographies...

Diaries and biographies have similarities, but they're for different audiences and purposes. Make sure you understand the differences between them, and apply that knowledge to your answer when you're in the exam.

Travel Writing

Travel writing needs to really convey your feelings about the place you're writing about.

Travel writing is personal and informal

1) Travel writing is an <u>account</u> of a writer's travels to a specific <u>place</u>.

2) If you're asked to produce some travel writing, you'll need to convey your <u>thoughts</u> and <u>opinions</u> about the place you're writing about, as well as give some <u>information</u> about it.

3) A piece of travel writing can <u>entertain</u> the reader (e.g. if it's in a book or magazine), <u>inform</u> them (e.g. if it's in a travel guide), or <u>persuade</u> them to visit a destination.

4) However, it's usually written for a <u>combination</u> of these purposes, e.g. <u>travel guides</u> are often written to both <u>inform</u> and <u>entertain</u> the reader.

5) Travel writing usually has an <u>informal</u> register and a <u>chatty</u> style, and it's almost always written in the <u>first person</u>. Try to write as if you're having a <u>conversation</u> with the audience, but don't forget to use lots of <u>descriptive techniques</u> too.

© iStockphoto.com/Miguel Angelo Silva

The travel brochure had failed to specify exactly what they meant by "transport included".

Use interesting language to convey your opinions

Imagine you have just visited New York.

Write an article about your trip for a travel magazine. Your article should include descriptions of the city and your own opinions.

> I've travelled to many cities during my career as a travel writer, and it's fair to say that there are a few I'd rather have avoided. None, however, have quite matched up to the levels of discomfort, disappointment and sheer frustration I experienced in the city of New York.
>
> I suspect my high expectations didn't help. Before embarking on my trip, I'd been regaled with stories from friends and family of gleaming, soaring skyscrapers and the vibrant, bustling streets of downtown Manhattan. "It's the best city in the world!" I was told.
>
> What I realised instead, somewhere between my fifth cup of overpriced coffee and my fourteenth hour-long queue, was that New York is the city of nightmares. Not only did it feel like the world's busiest city, it felt like the noisiest, too; by the end of my week there I found myself longing for the joys of silence and solitude. Maybe for some, New York is a city where dreams come true, but it was certainly far from the inspiring haven I had hoped to find.

This question asks you to write a magazine article. It needs to be entertaining and informative, and could also persuade the reader to agree with your point of view.

Use personal pronouns like 'I' to make the tone of your writing more personal.

Make your opinion on the city very clear.

Try to use all five senses to create a sense of the atmosphere of the place.

Use interesting language to make your text more entertaining.

Travel left-ing...   *...Travel right-ing*

You don't necessarily have to sing the praises of the place you're writing about. It's fine to have a negative opinion, as long as you express it clearly and use the appropriate language, tone and style for your audience.

Writing Reports and Essays

Reports and essays use a similar tone and style, but they do have one difference. Read on for the big reveal...

Reports and essays are similar

1) Reports and essays should be <u>impersonal</u> and <u>objective</u> in tone — you'll need to go through the arguments <u>for</u> and <u>against</u> something, then come to a conclusion that demonstrates your <u>own point of view</u>.

2) Reports and essays should follow a <u>logical structure</u>. They need to have:

   - An <u>introduction</u> that sets up the <u>main theme</u>.
   - Well-structured <u>paragraphs</u> covering the <u>strengths</u> and <u>weaknesses</u> of the arguments.
   - A <u>conclusion</u> that ties things together and offers <u>your own</u> point of view.

3) The purpose of reports and essays is almost always to <u>inform</u>, but they often <u>advise</u> their audience too.

4) You need to make sure you write for the correct <u>audience</u> — <u>essays</u> usually have quite a <u>general</u> audience, but <u>reports</u> are normally written for a <u>particular</u> person or group of people.

Reports should analyse and advise

Your school has a certain budget for extra-curricular activities. This year, they have a small amount of money left over, and they are deciding whether to award it to the rock-climbing club or the film society.

Write a report for the board of governors in which you discuss the options and make a recommendation of what you think they should do.

A Report Into The Possible Uses Of The Extra-Curricular Budget

By: John Coughton

Prepared For: Board of Governors

Date: 21st April 2015

This report has been commissioned by the board of governors to identify the best use of the funds available for extra-curricular activities at St. Swithins Park Secondary School. Two options have been investigated: the rock-climbing club and the film society. After careful consideration of the evidence collected from various interviews and data analysis, the conclusion has been reached that the film club is the most logical recipient of the excess funds.

On the one hand, the rock-climbing club appears to be the most obvious choice as it is the most costly to run: the club organises frequent expeditions involving expensive equipment and high travel costs. Having said that, the club does charge a members' fee, which helps to alleviate some of this financial burden.

At the start, show that you are clearly aware of who your audience is.

You don't need to create any suspense — give your opinion in the introduction.

Phrases like 'on the one hand' show that you have thought about both sides of the argument.

Your language should be very formal and impersonal, but you still need to convey a viewpoint.

In the real answer, you would go on to include several more paragraphs and finish with a conclusion that gives advice.

My school reports certainly covered my weaknesses...

Reports and essays are pretty straightforward when it comes down to it — just make sure that you're being as objective, analytical and formal as possible. It may be a bit boring, but it's a perfect recipe for exam success.

Writing Reviews

Writing a review involves clearly giving your opinion about something. The audience are reading because they're genuinely interested in your opinion, so what you say goes. You have all the power. Mwa ha ha...

Reviews should entertain as well as inform

1) A <u>review</u> is a piece of writing that gives an <u>opinion</u> about how <u>good</u> something is — it might be a book, a piece of music or even an exhibition.

2) <u>Reviews</u> can appear in lots of <u>different</u> publications. If you have to write a review in the exam, the question will usually tell you <u>where</u> it's going to appear.

3) The <u>publication</u> where your review appears will affect what kind of <u>audience</u> you're writing for and <u>how</u> you write. For example, a film review for a teen magazine could be <u>funny</u> and <u>informal</u>, but a review of a Shakespeare play for a broadsheet newspaper should be <u>serious</u> and <u>informative</u>.

4) You should also pay attention to <u>purpose</u>. Your review could have <u>several</u> different purposes:

   - Your review needs to <u>entertain</u> the reader.

   - You also need to <u>inform</u> the reader about the thing you're reviewing, based on your <u>own opinion</u>.

   - You might also need to <u>advise</u> the reader whether or not to see or do the thing you're reviewing.

5) <u>Don't</u> get too hung up on <u>describing</u> everything in minute detail — it's much more important that you give your <u>opinion</u>. Just keep your review <u>engaging</u> by focusing on the <u>interesting bits</u> and using <u>sophisticated language</u>.

Your review needs to give an evaluation

Imagine you have been to a music concert.

Write a review for a broadsheet newspaper that gives your opinion of the concert.

Make your opinion clear from the start of the review.

Make sure your review is informative as well as entertaining.

This review is for a broadsheet newspaper, so make sure you adapt your writing appropriately — use a formal register with fairly complex language.

Use figurative language to make your review interesting.

'Music through the Millennium': A Feast for the Ears

From the moment the audience took their seats, the auditorium was buzzing with excitement, and they were not to be disappointed. This stunning collection of classical and contemporary pieces took the audience on an unforgettable journey through a thousand years of music, from the intense gloom and misery of funeral marches to the pounding excitement of percussion movements, and the intense joy of some truly superb symphonies. This was a sonic experience not to be missed: a congregation of musical heavyweights that each packed a punch strong enough to knock the emotional stuffing out of even the stoniest of hearts. From start to end, 'Music through the Millennium' was a true schooling in the stirring power of music.

I read an article about cheese once — it was a brie-view...

Reviews are quite a nice thing to write — they're all about your opinions, which means you can go to town on saying what you think. You should try to express your thoughts clearly, and in a way that entertains the reader.

Writing Speeches

A speech needs to be powerful and moving. You should aim to have an emotional effect on the people who are listening. See if you can reduce them to tears with your carefully crafted sermon. Go on, I dare you...

Speeches need to be dramatic and engaging

1) <u>Speeches</u> are often written to <u>argue</u> or <u>persuade</u>, so they need to have a <u>dramatic</u>, <u>emotional impact</u> on their audience.

2) One way to make a speech persuasive is to give it an effective <u>structure</u> — arrange your points so that they build <u>tension</u> throughout your answer, then end with an <u>emotive</u> or <u>exciting</u> climax.

3) You can use lots of <u>language techniques</u> to make your writing <u>engaging</u> and <u>persuasive</u>:

These accusations are hateful, hurtful and humiliating. → <u>Alliteration</u> and the use of a <u>list</u> of three adjectives make this <u>sound</u> strong and angry.

> Persuasive language techniques like these are known as rhetorical devices.

Surely we have no other option? The current situation is a disgrace! → <u>Rhetorical questions</u> and <u>exclamations</u> engage the reader and make your writing sound more like <u>spoken language</u>.

4) Remember that speeches are <u>spoken</u>, not read. Try to use techniques that are effective when they're spoken <u>out loud</u>.

Your speech should make people think

You have been asked to attend an animal welfare conference which is all about the practice of keeping animals in zoos.

Write a speech to be delivered at the conference, in which you explain your point of view on the issue.

Start off by addressing your listeners directly and announcing the reason for your speech — show that you've understood your purpose and audience.

Try to use lots of personal pronouns like 'I', 'you' and 'we' to engage your audience.

Ladies and gentlemen, I have called you here today to defend the practice of keeping animals in captivity. I believe that zoos represent a positive presence in this country. The vast majority of modern British zoos are focused on conservation and education. To my mind, these important values are worth preserving. It is essential that we give our youngsters a sense of awareness about the world around them. We must impress upon the youth of today the need to protect endangered species and habitats. Zoos can help us to do this. Modern zoos offer extensive opportunities for these kinds of educational experiences: there are interactive exhibitions, talks from conservationists and live question-and-answer forums that will help to educate our young people.

Zoos can help us inspire a generation with the importance of conservation. Zoos can help us raise awareness of environmental issues. Zoos can help us by providing a space in which we can work together to build a safer, greener and more ecologically friendly world.

Vary the lengths of your sentences to show pauses and emphasis.

The word 'must' creates a confident tone.

You could use repetition to increase the dramatic impact of your speech.

Use rhetorical devices like lists of three to make your argument sound more forceful.

Ladies, gentlemen, and assorted zoo animals...

There are loads of famous speeches throughout history — you could try looking at some of the techniques they use. Luckily for you, your speech doesn't have to impress a huge crowd of people, just a few picky examiners...

Section Four — English Language: Writing

Writing Letters

Letters are always addressed to a particular person or group of people. This means that they have very specific audiences, so it's super important that you tailor your letter to suit that audience...

Letters can be formal or informal

1) If you're asked to write a letter, look at the audience to see if you need to use a formal or informal register.

2) If the letter is to someone you don't know well, or to someone in a position of authority, keep it formal with a serious tone. This means you should:

Charlie had forgotten to include a formal sign-off in her letter.

- Use formal greetings (e.g. 'Dear Sir/Madam') and sign-offs (e.g. 'Yours sincerely' if you've used their name, 'Yours faithfully' if you haven't).

- Use Standard English and formal vocabulary, e.g. you could use phrases like 'In my opinion...' or 'I find this state of affairs...'.

3) If the letter is to a friend or relative, or someone your own age, you should use a more informal register and personal tone. This means you should:

- Start with your reader's name, e.g. 'Dear Jenny', and sign off with 'best wishes' or 'see you soon'.

- Assume the reader already knows certain things about you.

- Make sure you still write in Standard English (so no text speak or slang) and show the examiner that you can use interesting vocabulary and sentence structures.

Don't make your letter too chatty

A friend has written you a letter in which they say that international travel isn't worth the cost.

Write a letter replying to your friend, in which you explain your point of view on this statement.

Dear Matt,

It was great to hear from you in your last letter, although I can't help but disagree with what you say about travelling. I think the benefits of international travel far outweigh the costs! Travelling is amazing: it broadens the mind, adds to your wealth of experience and heightens your awareness of the world around you.

I know what you're thinking — that's all well and good, but it's cheaper to go on holiday in the UK, and you get similar benefits, too. Well, if you're not put off by the constant threat of drizzle, that may be the case. But I think it's worth spending a little bit more money (and with the rise of cheap flights, it is only a little bit) to avoid wasting your holidays hiding from the British rain.

This letter is to a friend, so you need to keep it informal, but make sure your writing is still good enough to impress the examiner.

Use phrases like this to show familiarity with the reader and that you've understood your audience.

Some punctuation, such as exclamation marks, can help to create a personal tone for your letter.

Colloquial phrases like this can also help to set the right tone for your letter.

Introducing a counter-argument, then contradicting it, can help to build up your argument.

A love letter has a very specific purpose and audience...

... but you probably won't be asked to write one in the exam. You will need to pay attention to purpose and audience though. Make sure your letter completes the task in the question and is written in an appropriate style.

Introduction to English Literature

It's time to get to grips with English Literature. You'll probably have to sit two exams — here's what to expect...

You'll study a range of texts for GCSE English Literature

1) If you're taking English Literature, you'll study a wide range of <u>poetry</u>, <u>prose</u> and <u>drama</u>. The texts you'll have to study, and answer questions on, are:

- a <u>Shakespeare play</u> — e.g. 'Macbeth', 'The Merchant of Venice'.
- a <u>novel</u> from the <u>19th century</u> — e.g. 'A Christmas Carol', 'Jane Eyre'.
- a modern (post-1914) <u>play</u> or <u>novel</u> — e.g. 'Blood Brothers', 'Animal Farm'.
- an anthology of <u>poetry</u> written between 1789 and now.

Sections Five, Six and Seven are full of advice on writing about prose and drama. Sections Eight and Nine will help you with poetry questions.

2) In the exam, you'll also have to write about one or two <u>unseen poems</u> — poems you <u>haven't studied</u> in class.

- For most exam boards there will be two <u>unseen poems</u> — you'll have to <u>analyse</u> and <u>compare</u> them.
- For other exam boards there might be a question on an <u>unseen poem</u> that you have to compare with a <u>poem</u> you <u>have studied</u>.

Section Ten is all about preparing for the unseen poetry part of your course.

3) For some exam boards, you might also get an extract from a <u>novel</u> or <u>play</u> you <u>haven't studied</u>, which you'll have to compare with a <u>text</u> you <u>have</u> studied. Ask your <u>teacher</u> exactly what you'll have to do in the exam.

The assessment objectives cover different skills

The <u>assessment objectives</u> cover all the things you need to do to get a <u>good grade</u> in the exams. They are:

AO 1
- Give your own <u>thoughts</u> and <u>opinions</u> on the text.
- <u>Back up</u> your interpretations using <u>evidence</u> from the text (e.g. quotes).

AO 2
- <u>Explain</u> how writers use <u>language</u>, <u>structure</u> and <u>form</u>, and what <u>effect</u> this has on the reader.
- Use <u>technical terms</u> to support your analysis.

AO 3
- Show that you understand how the text relates to the <u>context</u> in which it was written or set.

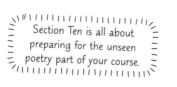

AO3 and AO4 aren't assessed on every question — check with your teacher if you want to know where they're assessed.

AO 4
- Use a range of <u>sentence structures</u> and <u>vocabulary</u>, so that your writing is <u>clear</u> and <u>effective</u>.
- Write <u>accurately</u>, paying particular attention to spelling, punctuation and grammar.
- AO4 counts for <u>5%</u> of your <u>overall mark</u> — flick to <u>Section Eleven</u> for advice on writing well.

Stifling office, lovely summer's day — the context this was written in...

You don't need to memorise these assessment objectives — they're just to give you an idea of the things you need to think about when you're revising. Of course, if you <u>want</u> to memorise them, that's entirely up to you...

Introduction to English Literature

Writing about Prose and Drama

Prose and drama are similar in lots of ways, so this section covers some of the common features found in the two types of text. Then, Sections Six (drama) and Seven (prose) deal with issues specific to each type of writing.

Questions could be about themes, characters or settings

1) Read the question <u>carefully</u> to make sure you're clear on <u>what</u> the question is asking you to focus on. This could be:

- the personality of a character
- a specific mood or atmosphere
- a specific theme or message
- attitudes towards a theme or issue
- relationships between characters

2) Here are some <u>examples</u> of the <u>types</u> of question that might come up in the exam:

How does Stevenson present the theme of reputation?

This question asks you to focus on the theme of reputation.

This is a character-based question — it asks you to analyse the character of Eric.

Explore how the character of Eric changes through the play.

3) Most questions will ask you to <u>comment</u> on <u>how</u> the writer <u>presents</u> something to the reader. This means that you need to focus on <u>language</u>, <u>structure</u> and <u>form</u>.

'How' questions want you to think about the writer's techniques and use of literary features.

This is the focus of the question — you need to use a range of examples from the text to support your answer.

Authors use language, structure and form to present things.

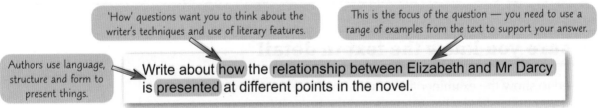

Write about how the relationship between Elizabeth and Mr Darcy is presented at different points in the novel.

Some questions ask about an extract from the text

1) The exam question might ask you to focus on the <u>whole text</u>, an <u>extract</u> from the text, or <u>both</u>.

2) If you're asked to write about an extract, it's <u>doubly important</u> to focus on things like <u>language</u>, <u>structure</u> and <u>form</u>. The examiner knows that you've got the text in front of you, so they're expecting you to <u>pick out</u> and <u>explain</u> some of the features in it.

You could get a question asking you to compare an extract from the text you've studied with an extract from a different text. Make sure you read the instructions carefully.

3) Here are some <u>examples</u> of the <u>type</u> of question that might come up:

It's clear that you need to focus only on the extract. Don't make any points about the rest of the text.

Write about the presentation of childhood in this extract.

Focus only on the extract below rather than the rest of the text you've studied.

This means that you need to explore how the theme is presented in the extract <u>and</u> in the rest of the text.

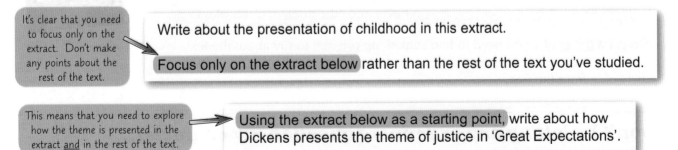

Using the extract below as a starting point, write about how Dickens presents the theme of justice in 'Great Expectations'.

Writing about Prose and Drama

Make sure you answer the question you're given

1) It's important to focus on the <u>question</u> — read it <u>carefully</u> a couple of times <u>before</u> planning your answer.

2) Some questions might give you <u>bullet points</u> of things to consider when writing your essay.
If there <u>aren't</u> any bullet points, then it might be useful to <u>write</u> some of your <u>own</u>, for example:

> Explore how Brontë presents the character of Mrs Reed in 'Jane Eyre'.
>
> - *What does Mrs Reed say and do in the novel?*   - *How does she treat other characters?*
> - *How does Brontë want the reader to feel about Mrs Reed? How does she achieve this?*

3) Make sure <u>everything</u> you write in your essay <u>answers the question</u>
— irrelevant points <u>won't</u> get you any <u>marks</u>.

Mrs Reed is Jane's aunt. She lives at Gateshead Hall with her children: John, Eliza and Georgiana. →	This is <u>too general</u> — it doesn't tell you anything about <u>how</u> Brontë presents the character of Mrs Reed.
Brontë presents Mrs Reed as a stern, bitter character, who treats the young Jane with "miserable cruelty". →	This is much better — it <u>comments</u> on the <u>presentation</u> of Mrs Reed's character and includes a <u>quote</u> from the text to support the point.

Make sure you know the text in detail

See pages 39-40 for more on writing about characters.

1) You need to show the examiner that you know the text <u>really well</u>, and that you understand <u>what happens</u> and the <u>order</u> it happens in.

2) Make sure you're familiar with <u>all</u> the <u>characters</u> in the text — the examiner will be impressed if you make references to the <u>minor characters</u> as well as the major ones.

3) Learn some key <u>quotes</u> from the text that you can use in your essay to <u>support</u> your points.

Introduce some of your own ideas

1) Write about your <u>personal response</u> to the text. Think about what <u>emotions</u> it evokes and whether you <u>like</u> or <u>empathise</u> with certain characters.

The reader feels sympathetic towards Pip as he reads the names of his dead parents on the gravestone. →	Don't use "I" when you're talking about your personal response — use "<u>the reader</u>" when you're writing about a novel and "<u>the audience</u>" for plays.

Dad could usually tell from Harriet's face when she'd had an original idea.

2) To get a <u>top grade</u>, you need to find something <u>original</u> to say about the text. You can make whatever point you like, as long as you can <u>back it up</u> with <u>evidence</u> from the text.

I won't be letting any examiners question my character...

... I'm a charming, witty, sophisticated adult — honest. Anyway, whatever question is on your exam, make sure you read it carefully, plan out your answer to it, and focus on features of language, structure and form.

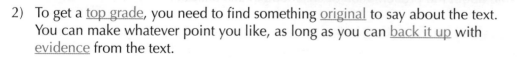

Section Five — English Literature: Prose and Drama

Writing about Characters

You need to know about something called 'characterisation' — this means the methods that an author uses to convey information about, or make the reader feel a certain way about, a character in the text.

Characters are always there for a reason

1) When you're answering a question about a character, bear in mind that characters always have a purpose.

2) This means that you can't talk about them as if they're real people — make it clear that the author has created them to help get a message across.

3) A character's appearance, actions and language all help to get this message across.

Find bits where the writer describes the characters

Find descriptions of how they look or act, and then think about what this might say about them.

> In 'Lord of the Flies', Golding's description of Jack's face as "crumpled" and "ugly without silliness" implies that he might have a sinister and unpleasant personality.

Examine the characters' actions

1) Look at what characters do, and then consider what that says about them.

2) Try to work out why a character does something. Most characters are motivated by a variety of things, but there's usually one main driving force behind what they do.

> The fact that Utterson spends hours waiting for Hyde outside Jekyll's back door shows his care for his friend, but also his inquisitive nature.

> Tybalt's confrontational and violent actions (e.g. stabbing Mercutio) are ultimately driven by his fierce loyalty to the Capulets.

Look at the way characters speak

1) The way characters, including the narrator, speak tells you a lot about them.

2) Remember to think about why the author is making their characters speak the way they do. Think about how the author wants you, the reader, to perceive the character.

> In 'An Inspector Calls', Birling repeatedly shouts "Rubbish!" to dismiss what other people have said. But he finishes his own sentences with "of course", to make his own claims seem obvious and matter-of-fact. This means that the audience perceives him to be arrogant and opinionated.

Look at how the characters treat other people

The writer can tell you a lot about their characters by showing you how they get on with others. It can reveal sides to their character that they keep hidden from the other main characters.

> My rage was without bounds; I sprang on him, impelled by all the feelings which can arm one being against the existence of another.

> In 'Frankenstein', Victor is kind and polite to most of the characters in the novel, but his attack on the monster reveals his concealed anger and violence.

Section Five — English Literature: Prose and Drama

Writing about Characters

Make sure you're prepared for character questions

Characters are key elements of any text, so it's not really a surprise that examiners enjoy asking about them in exams. Here are some important questions to think about when you're studying or revising characters:

Why is the character important?

- How do they affect the plot?
- Do they represent a particular point of view?
- What would happen if they weren't there?

→ *Madame is a key character in 'Never Let Me Go' — she provides a link with the world outside Hailsham, and her apparent disgust with the children hints at the wider world's perception of them.*

Does the character change over the course of the story?

- Does their personality change?
- Does their behaviour change?
- Are the changes positive or negative?

→ *Benedick changes over the course of 'Much Ado About Nothing'. He is initially independent, insulting and full of bravado, but his character becomes more gentle and endearing as his love for Beatrice grows.*

What has the character learnt by the end of the text?

- Does the character learn anything?
- Do the character's opinions change?
- How do these changes affect the character?

→ *Ebenezer Scrooge learns to be charitable, generous and empathetic thanks to his experiences with the ghosts in 'A Christmas Carol'.*

How does the writer reveal the character's personality?

- How are the character's actions and experiences presented to the reader?
- Is the reader's view of the character the same as other characters' view of them?

→ *The cold-hearted nature of Estella in 'Great Expectations' is revealed by her frequent attempts to "deceive and entrap" men. The reader is able to see her true nature more clearly than Pip, who is blinded by his love for her.*

How is the character similar or different to other characters?

- How does the character relate to other characters?
- Do differences between characters impact on the plot?
- What is the writer showing us through these differences?

→ *In some ways, Linda turns into Mrs Johnstone in 'Blood Brothers', becoming a housewife at a young age whilst also having to provide for the family.*

Does the reader like or sympathise with the character?

- Why does the reader feel that way about the character?
- How does the writer shape the reader's feelings about the character?
- How does the reader's opinion of the character affect their opinion of the text as a whole?

→ *The reader sympathises with Meena in 'Anita and Me' because her loyalty and trust is betrayed by Anita. Having the narrative in Meena's voice helps create empathy, as it means that Meena's viewpoint is heard throughout.*

It'll take a tough character to survive all those questions...

There's no way of knowing what will appear on your exam, but revising key characters is an excellent way of preparing. Don't forget about the minor characters too — think about what they contribute to the text.

The Writer's Techniques

There are lots of marks available in English Literature for commenting on the way writers use language. If you don't believe me, well, I'm not sure why you're reading this book...

Analysing the writer's use of language is key

1) Writers select the language they use carefully — it's up to you to work out why they've chosen a particular word or phrase, and to explain the effect that it has.

2) Look out for any interesting, unusual or specialist vocabulary — think about why it's been used. Take note of any repeated words and phrases too — they will have been repeated for a reason.

3) Examining the language used by characters is really important — think about the way characters speak, why they speak in that way and whether the way they speak is different to other characters.

"D' they call y' Eddie?" "Gis a sweet"	In 'Blood Brothers', Russell uses informal, colloquial language for the Johnstone family — they omit letters off the end of words and use non-standard pronouns. This language is used to reflect their social class.

Hyde speaks "with a flush of anger" and makes inhuman noises, e.g. he screams in "animal terror".	In 'Dr Jekyll and Mr Hyde', Stevenson uses language to reinforce Hyde's incivility — Hyde doesn't speak as gentlemen were expected to, suggesting to other characters that something is wrong.

Look out for imagery

Imagery is particularly common in prose texts, but it does crop up in plays too — Shakespeare uses lots of it.

1) Imagery is when an author uses language to create a picture in the reader's mind, or to describe something more vividly. It can add to the reader's or the audience's understanding of the story.

2) Similes describe something by saying that it's like something else:

No one can conceive the variety of feelings which bore me onwards, like a hurricane, in the first enthusiasm of success.	In 'Frankenstein', Shelley uses the simile "like a hurricane" to emphasise the power of Victor's feelings.

3) Metaphors describe something by saying it is something else:

The instruments of darkness tell us truths	In 'Macbeth', Banquo's suspicion of the Witches is shown by his use of the metaphor "instruments of darkness" to describe them.

4) Personification describes something (e.g. an animal, object or aspect of nature) as if it were human.

It was a wild, cold, seasonable night of March, with a pale moon, lying on her back...	In 'Dr Jekyll and Mr Hyde', The personification of the moon makes it seem that the whole world has been turned upside down by Jekyll's secret.

Comment on sentence structure

1) It's not just particular words and phrases that you can comment on — you should also look at how writers use sentences and paragraphs to reinforce their points.

2) Different sentence lengths create different effects, e.g. a succession of short sentences could build tension or excitement, whereas long sentences might show a character getting carried away with their emotions.

The Writer's Techniques

Pay attention to descriptions and settings

1) Writers use <u>settings</u> to influence the way you <u>feel</u> about what's happening.

2) In the exam, you could get a passage that <u>describes</u> one of the settings from the text and be asked to talk about how the author has used it to create <u>atmosphere</u>.

3) You need to look at the writer's <u>descriptions</u> and think about <u>why</u> they have been included and <u>what effect</u> they have.

> *Alleys and archways, like so many cesspools, disgorged their offences of smell, and dirt, and life, upon the straggling streets* ⟹ In 'A Christmas Carol', Dickens uses descriptive language to present his reader with a <u>realistic</u>, <u>harsh</u> vision of <u>poverty</u> in London.

> *I did not dare return to the apartment which I inhabited, but felt impelled to hurry on, although drenched by the rain which poured from a black and comfortless sky.* ⟹ In 'Frankenstein', this <u>bleak</u> setting reflects Victor's <u>hopeless and gloomy mood</u>.

Writers can present their ideas using symbolism

1) Symbols can be used to reinforce the <u>themes</u> that run through a text. Look out for things that could be a <u>symbol</u> for something else, e.g. a <u>thunderstorm</u> could be a symbol for <u>destruction</u>.

> *In 'An Inspector Calls', Priestley uses Eva Smith as a symbol. Her first name sounds like 'Eve', the first woman (in the Biblical account of creation), which suggests she symbolises all women. Her surname is very common and it's also the word for a tradesman, which implies that she represents all ordinary, working-class women.*

2) Symbols are often used to create <u>additional meanings</u>. If the literal meaning of a sentence sounds strange, try to work out whether there's another layer of meaning.

> *This boy is Ignorance. This girl is Want. Beware them both* ⟹ In 'A Christmas Carol', the characters of Ignorance and Want <u>symbolise</u> the <u>problems</u> caused by society's neglect of the <u>poor</u>.

Structure is always important

1) <u>Structure</u> is the <u>order</u> that events happen in. Make sure you think about how a writer has put a text together, and what the <u>effect</u> of this is.

2) Structural devices can be used to make a text more <u>interesting</u>. For example:

- <u>foreshadowing</u> gives <u>hints</u> about what will happen <u>later on</u> in the story.

- <u>flashbacks</u> temporarily <u>shift</u> the story back in time, often showing something from the <u>past</u> that is significant in the <u>present</u>.

There's more information about the structure of plays on p.46 and prose texts on p.49.

> *The opening of 'The History Boys' shows Irwin in a wheelchair, before Bennett moves time backwards twenty years and Irwin is able to walk. The audience is therefore left wondering what happens to Irwin and expects that something is going to occur during the course of the play to explain his disability.*

I'd much rather analyse the writer's use of pictures...

... but sadly I didn't see that mentioned in the Assessment Objectives. The only picture in most of these texts is on the front cover, so you're going to have to look at language and structure if you want to get any marks.

Section Five — English Literature: Prose and Drama

Context and the Writer's Message

Texts are influenced by the time and place they're written and set in, as well as by the person who wrote them. You need to consider these influences and think about whether the writer is trying to convey a certain message.

Make sure you're familiar with the context of the text

1) You need to know roughly <u>when</u> the text was <u>written</u>, and what <u>impact</u> this has on <u>how</u> the text was written and how certain <u>issues</u> are <u>portrayed</u> in the text.

2) Show the examiner that you're aware of the <u>wider issues</u> raised by the text, and <u>comment</u> on them.

3) Here are some of the <u>issues</u> that you should look out for:

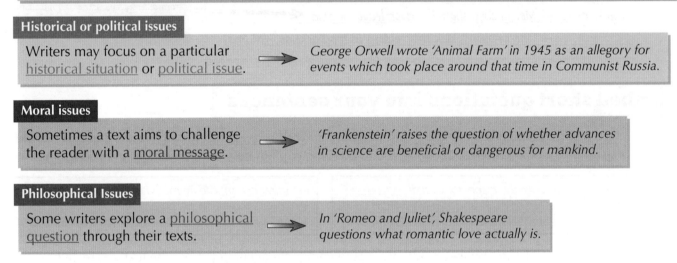

Social or cultural issues

Authors often <u>comment</u> on the <u>society</u> they're living in, particularly the <u>faults</u> they associate with it. ⟶ *'Blood Brothers' examines social class, and how it can determine the course of people's lives.*

Historical or political issues

Writers may focus on a particular <u>historical situation</u> or <u>political issue</u>. ⟶ *George Orwell wrote 'Animal Farm' in 1945 as an allegory for events which took place around that time in Communist Russia.*

Moral issues

Sometimes a text aims to challenge the reader with a <u>moral message</u>. ⟶ *'Frankenstein' raises the question of whether advances in science are beneficial or dangerous for mankind.*

Philosophical Issues

Some writers explore a <u>philosophical question</u> through their texts. ⟶ *In 'Romeo and Juliet', Shakespeare questions what romantic love actually is.*

Think about the major issues the text deals with

1) Texts usually have something to say about the <u>society</u> in which they were <u>written</u> or <u>set</u>.

2) Think carefully about the <u>themes</u> of the text, and what the writer might have been <u>saying</u> about them.

Fate	**Gender**	**Social Class**	**Ambition**
Do we control our own lives?	What is the impact of gender inequality?	Is it right that social class is so important?	Is ambition healthy or destructive?

3) It's also useful to think about what the writer's <u>overall message</u> is. Think about <u>why</u> they might have <u>written</u> the book, and look at the <u>issues</u> and <u>questions</u> the text raises.

Dickens's message in 'A Christmas Carol' is that the rich have a duty to help those less fortunate than themselves.

The central message of 'Lord of the Flies' is that all humans have evil inside them and are capable of committing terrible deeds.

Focus on the content of this book — the context is pretty dull...

You need to be familiar with the content and the context of the texts you're studying. Questions that focus just on context are very rare, but you should look for opportunities to include some of your wider knowledge.

Using Quotations

You're not allowed to take any of your texts into the exam, so you're going to need to learn some quotations...

Learn key quotations that are relevant to characters and themes

1) When you're reading a text, make a note of some good quotes to learn. Examiners aren't expecting you to memorise big chunks of text, so the quotes you pick out should be short and snappy.

2) You need to use the quotes to back up the points in your essay, so make sure the quotes you choose are relevant to things you're likely to write about in the exam, e.g. a key character, theme or technique.

3) When you're revising, it's a good idea to make lists of key quotes for each theme or character.

> 'ANITA AND ME': THEME — FAMILY
> The Rutters — "Tell me mom. I don't care." (Anita)
> — "Where's me mum?" (Tracey)
> The Kumars — Meena says she will "never leave" Mama
> — "the English... kick their elders in the backside" (Mama)

It's a good idea to learn quotes that relate to different aspects of a theme — in this example there are some quotes from different characters. Quotes can be as short as a word or phrase — don't try to learn long sentences.

Embed short quotations into your sentences

1) The best way to use quotes is to embed (insert) them into your sentences. This just means that they should be a natural part of a sentence, allowing you to go on to explain how the quote supports your point.

> In 'An Inspector Calls', the Inspector describes Eva positively, calling her "pretty" and "lively", which makes the audience feel more sympathetic towards her.

> In 'Animal Farm', the animals' lack of power is revealed by Boxer's repetition of "Napoleon is always right", which shows that he can no longer think for himself.

2) If you get an extract question (see p.37), make sure you quote accurately from the text you're given. But don't be tempted to quote huge chunks of text — always be selective with the quotes you use and make sure you explain their significance or effect.

Quoting Shakespeare is slightly different

Writing about Shakespearean texts is covered in more detail on pages 47-48.

1) The way you quote something from Shakespeare differs slightly depending on whether the lines are in prose or verse (poetry). If each new line of the text starts with a capital letter, it's verse, but if a new line just carries on from the previous line without a capital letter, it's prose.

2) If it's prose, then just quote as you would do from a novel.

3) If it's verse, then you need to be careful about line breaks. If you quote something that goes over more than one line in the original text, you need to show this using a slash — '/'.

> In 'Macbeth', the Witches speak in rhyming couplets, for example, "When the hurly-burly's done, / When the battle's lost and won." This makes their speech sound unnatural and mysterious.

This answer uses a quote that's in verse and goes over two lines, so it uses a '/' to show where the line break is in the original text.

Quoting Shakespeare made me the man I am today...

"You have such a February face, so full of frost, of storm and cloudiness!" ('Much Ado About Nothing') — see what I mean? Anyway, make sure to learn plenty of (relevant) quotes for the exams — your essays need them.

Reading Plays

That's enough playing around with prose — this section just focuses on the dramatic elements of GCSE English.

Stage directions describe the action on stage

Stage directions are usually written in italics or put in brackets to distinguish them from things that are said.

1) When you're reading a play, look out for the stage directions. These are instructions from the playwright to the director and the actors — they can tell you a lot about how the playwright wants the play to be performed.

2) There are lots of things to look out for in the stage directions. For example, music and sound effects might be used to create a specific mood, or the set may be designed to create a certain atmosphere. Stage directions can also describe the characters' actions and the use of props.

3) You should write about how the stage directions reveal the playwright's intentions.

Staging

The dining-room of a fairly large suburban house... It has good solid furniture... *'An Inspector Calls' — J.B. Priestley* ⟶	In these opening stage directions, Priestley establishes how he would like the set to look. The set reflects the class and status of the Birlings.

Action

We see Mickey comb the town, breaking through groups of people, looking, searching, desperate... *'Blood Brothers' — Willy Russell* ⟶	These stage directions describe what's happening on stage — Mickey's desperate search makes this scene dramatic.

Dialogue

Irwin *(thoughtfully) That's very true.* *'The History Boys' — Alan Bennett* ⟶	The stage direction here tells the actor playing Irwin how he should deliver his line.

Plays contain different types of speech

1) Dialogue is when two or more characters are speaking. It shows how characters interact with each other.

Eric *If you think that's the best she can do —* **Sheila** *Don't be an ass, Eric.* **Mrs Birling** *Now stop it, you two.* ⟶	This dialogue from 'An Inspector Calls' hints at the tensions that exist between the characters.

2) A monologue is when one character speaks and the other characters on stage listen to them.

3) In a soliloquy, a single character speaks their thoughts out loud — other characters can't hear them. This reveals to the audience something of the character's inner thoughts and feelings.

4) An aside is like a soliloquy, but it is usually a shorter comment which is only heard by the audience — other characters don't hear it.

Macbeth *(aside) Glamis, and Thane of Cawdor:* *The greatest is behind. (To Rosse and Angus)* ⟶ *Thanks for your pains.*	Macbeth's first remarks are heard only by the audience, then he returns to addressing other characters.

CGP editor (wearing a comedy bow-tie): "Read this page carefully..."

Stage directions can tell you all sorts of things about characters, themes, the writer's attitudes or the play as a whole. Don't just skip over them when you're reading a play — try to work out what they're there for.

Writing about Drama

When you're writing about a play, always keep in mind the fact that it's intended to be watched by an audience.

Write about the style of the play

1) You need to write in <u>detail</u> about the <u>language</u> used in the play. Think about:

> - The <u>effects</u> of the language used, e.g. whether it creates suspense, humour, anger...
> - Any <u>imagery</u> that's used, e.g. similes, metaphors and personification (see p.41).
> - How playwrights use <u>dialogue</u>, e.g. to develop characters, reveal the <u>plot</u> and explore <u>wider issues</u> and <u>themes</u>.

2) You also need to think about how the play is <u>structured</u>. For example:

> - How does the playwright use <u>act</u> and <u>scene breaks</u>?
>   *For example, each act of 'An Inspector Calls' ends on a <u>cliffhanger</u>, and at the beginning of the next act, the "<u>scene and situation</u> are <u>exactly</u> as they <u>were</u>" at the end of the previous act. This builds the <u>tension</u> and sense of <u>pressure</u> that the Birlings are under.*
> - How does the playwright show <u>changes</u> in <u>time</u>?
>   *For example, in 'Blood Brothers', Russell uses a <u>montage</u> (a series of short scenes) to move time forwards <u>four years</u>. The <u>speed</u> at which time passes on stage <u>symbolises</u> the <u>fleetingness of youth</u>, and gives the audience the sense that the play is moving rapidly towards its <u>tragic ending</u>.*

Show you know that plays are intended to be watched not read

1) Plays are written to be <u>acted on stage</u>, not read silently from a book. This means that you shouldn't refer to the '<u>reader</u>' — talk about the '<u>audience</u>' instead.

> *Siobhan acts as a kind of narrator in 'The Curious Incident of the Dog in the Night-Time' — she reads segments of Christopher's work, which helps the audience make sense of what's happening, and gives them an insight into Christopher's mind.*
>
> ⟹ You should comment on how the play works on <u>stage</u> and how this <u>impacts</u> on the <u>audience</u>.

2) You also need to show that you appreciate the writer's <u>stagecraft</u> — their <u>skill</u> at writing for the <u>stage</u>. Playwrights use features like <u>silences</u>, <u>actions</u> and <u>sound effects</u> to create a mood, reveal something in a certain way or add drama to a situation — these things are usually mentioned in <u>stage directions</u> (see p.45).

3) Appreciating the stagecraft means asking yourself a few <u>key questions</u>:

- How would this scene <u>look on stage</u>?   • How would the <u>audience react</u>?   • Is it <u>effective</u>?

4) For example, in Act Two of 'Blood Brothers', Russell uses <u>simultaneous conversations</u> to create a fast-paced scene:

> *Mickey and Sammy are speaking on one side of the stage whilst Edward and Linda are speaking on the other side. Both conversations have life-changing consequences, and the combination of the two dialogues emphasises the fact that both twins are at a crossroads in their lives.*

Whatever you do, don't make a scene in the exam...

Playwrights have the audience in mind when writing plays, so if you can do the same in your essays then you'll be well on the way to writing a top answer. Don't forget to think about the play's wider issues and themes too.

Writing About Shakespeare

There's no escaping the Bard of Avon — love him or hate him, you've got to study him.

Shakespeare's plays can be serious or funny

Make sure you're clear on the genre of the play you're studying:

Tragedy

1) Tragedies (e.g. 'Macbeth', 'Romeo and Juliet') often focus on big topics — e.g. love, death, war, religion. They are usually about the sad or terrible downfall of the main character.

2) Tragedies can be moving and often have a moral message.

3) Some of Shakespeare's tragedies are set in an imaginary or historical world. The characters are often kings, queens or other rulers.

Comedy

1) Comedies (e.g. 'Much Ado About Nothing', 'The Merchant of Venice') are written to make the audience laugh.

2) Events and characters are often silly and exaggerated.

3) Comedies can still have a moral message though.

© iStockphoto.com/alblec

Joseph's act had the potential to be both comic and tragic.

Shakespeare also wrote history plays (e.g. 'Henry V'). These plays are based on real historical events.

Show you're aware that Shakespeare was writing 400 years ago

1) Shakespeare (1564-1616) wrote his plays about 400 years ago, so it's not surprising that some of the language, themes and ideas can seem a bit strange to us.

2) He lived at the end of a period of European history known as the Renaissance — a time when there were lots of developments in the arts, politics, religion and science. The theatre was very popular at this time.

3) Many people in Shakespeare's Britain believed in the supernatural — people were executed for witchcraft, and superstitious behaviour was common. Several of Shakespeare's plays have supernatural elements, e.g. the Witches in 'Macbeth' and the spirits in 'The Tempest'. The audience would usually have taken these supernatural characters seriously.

4) Knowing a bit about theatrical performances in Shakespeare's time will help you to write top answers about his plays. Here are some of the key features:

- Only men were allowed to act on stage — all the female roles were played by boys. Shakespeare's comedies include lots of jokes about girls dressing up as boys.

- Most of the actors wore elaborate costumes that were based on the fashions of when the play was written, and that reflected the status of the character. Plays set overseas, e.g. in ancient Rome or Greece, used costumes appropriate to the location.

- Musicians helped to create atmosphere in the theatre. They also made sound effects, such as the thunder at the beginning of 'Macbeth'.

- Plays didn't use much scenery — sets were simple so that they could show different locations in a play, and could be adapted easily to be used for several different plays.

The early 17th century — not exactly a vintage period for actresses...

It wasn't until 1660 that women were allowed to act on stage in England — when Shakespeare wrote his plays, he would have been expecting all the female characters to be played by boys and young men. Crazy.

Section Six — English Literature: Drama

Shakespeare's Language

Shakespeare's language can be a bit daunting, but if you study it carefully you'll be able to understand it.

Be specific when you write about language

When you're writing about a Shakespeare play, you need to take a close look at the language, and think about the effect it would have on someone watching the play. Here are a few things to look out for:

1) Imagery, including similes, metaphors and personification.

There the grown serpent lies; the worm that's fled *Hath nature that in time will venom breed* *'Macbeth' Act 3, Scene 4*	Macbeth uses metaphors to describe the dead Banquo as a "serpent", and Fleance (Banquo's son) as a "worm". He's worried about Fleance because the Witches prophesied that Banquo's descendants would be kings.

2) Striking words and phrases — when you read through the text, make a note of any words that jump out at you. Think about why they're important, and what effect they have.

If you tickle us, do we not laugh? If you poison us, do *we not die? And if you wrong us, shall we not revenge?* *'The Merchant of Venice' Act 3, Scene 1*	Shylock's emotive speech uses rhetorical questions to show that as a Jew he's no different to Christians. The mention of revenge hints at his anger.

3) Humour — Shakespeare uses lots of puns and jokes.

Ask for me tomorrow, and you shall *find me a grave man.* *'Romeo and Juliet' Act 3, Scene 1*	Mercutio makes a joke about his own death, playing on the double meaning of "grave" ('serious', and 'a place to put dead bodies').

Look out for switches between verse and prose

Shakespeare wrote his plays in a mixture of poetry and prose.
You can tell a lot about a character by looking at the way they speak.

> A line written using iambic pentameter (see p.55) usually has 10 syllables (five unstressed and five stressed).

If music be the food of love, play on; *Give me excess of it, that, surfeiting,* *The appetite may sicken, and so die.* *'Twelfth Night' Act 1, Scene 1*	The majority of Shakespeare's lines are written in blank verse (unrhymed iambic pentameter). Blank verse sounds grander than prose and can be used by almost any characters, but lower-class, comic and mad characters generally don't use it.

From forth the fatal loins of these two foes *A pair of star-cross'd lovers take their life,* *Whose misadventur'd piteous overthrows* *Doth with their death bury their parents' strife.* *'Romeo and Juliet' Prologue*	Sometimes Shakespeare uses rhymed iambic pentameter to make speech sound dramatic and impressive, e.g. at the beginning and end of a scene, or when a posh character is speaking.

Come hither, neighbour Seacole. God hath blest you *with a good name: to be a well-favoured man is the* *gift of fortune, but to write and read comes by nature.* *'Much Ado About Nothing' Act 3, Scene 3*	The rest of Shakespeare's writing is in normal prose. Funny bits and dialogue between more minor or lower-class characters are usually written in prose.

Don't switch between writing in prose and verse in the exam...

Writing essays in rhymed iambic pentameter is not advisable — trust me. Whenever you write about a feature of Shakespeare's language, make sure you explain the effect it has — that's where the marks are.

Writing about Prose

You should be fairly familiar with the concept of reading prose — in fact, you're doing it right now...

Structure is how the writer puts the text together

1) Writers work hard to present and communicate their ideas effectively. Your challenge is to work out why they've structured their novel in a certain way and what the effect of their decisions is.

2) Here are some questions to help you think about structure:

- Is the novel split into chapters or sections? What is the effect of this — e.g. does it create cliffhangers or switch the focus of the plot?

- How does the novel start and end? What is the impact of this on the reader?

- Does the plot move forwards chronologically (in time order)? Or does the time change — e.g. by using flashbacks?

- Are there any examples of foreshadowing (where the author hints about future events)?

- Is there one main plot, or are there several plots that link together?

- Does the author use any other specific structural devices — e.g. a frame narrative (where the main story is told within the frame of another story), or embedded narratives (where several different stories are told within the main story)?

Comment on the writer's choice of language

It takes some choice language to make Pamel get up in the morning.

1) Authors love using descriptive language, including similes, metaphors and personification, so look out for this and comment on why it's been used.

2) Particularly keep an eye out for any language or imagery that's repeated — there's usually a reason for this:

he locked the note into his safe *Utterson locked the door of his business room* *he turned to examine the door in the by-street. It was locked* →	In 'Dr Jekyll and Mr Hyde', there are numerous images of locked doors. These are used to symbolise secrecy, and the way that humans try to hide their dual nature.

3) The language used by characters is also really important. For example:

"Yow can come with uz, right, but don't say nothin'" →	In 'Anita and Me', Meena uses Midlands dialect words, slang and non-standard grammar to try to fit in and impress Anita.

"Be calm! I entreat you to hear me, before you give vent to your hatred on my devoted head. Have I not suffered enough that you seek to increase my misery?" →	The monster in 'Frankenstein' uses eloquent language. This makes him sound more human, so the reader empathises with him.

Bun-mayo-lettuce-burger-salsa-bun — that's my kind of structure...

First, stop drooling over the imaginary, perfectly-structured burger. Second, check back over the page to make sure you're happy with everything on it. Writing about a text's structure will really impress the examiner.

Analysing Characters and Narrators

I've said it before and I'll say it again — novels without any characters are just not worth reading...

Characters' thoughts are often described

There's lots more information about analysing characters on pages 39-40.

1) Novels and short stories give <u>descriptions</u> of characters' thoughts and behaviour — the narrator often informs you about what <u>characters</u> are <u>thinking</u>.

2) <u>Look out</u> for those bits, <u>quote</u> them, and comment on how they help answer the question.

The head, he thought, appeared to agree with him. Run away, said the head silently...

The narrator of 'Lord of the Flies' describes Simon's <u>thoughts</u> and <u>imagined conversation</u> with the pig's head. This allows the reader to experience Simon's <u>hallucinations</u>.

There are different types of narrator

1) All <u>prose</u> texts have a <u>narrator</u> — a <u>voice</u> that's telling the story.

2) A <u>first-person</u> narrator is a character who tells the story from their <u>perspective</u>, e.g. Pip narrates 'Great Expectations' and Kathy narrates 'Never Let Me Go'. You get a first-hand description of exactly what the character <u>sees</u>, <u>does</u> and <u>thinks</u> all the way through the story.

In what ecstasy of unhappiness I got these broken words out of myself, I don't know. The rhapsody welled up within me, like blood from an inward wound, and gushed out.

In 'Great Expectations', Pip's narration is very <u>personal</u> and appeals to the reader's <u>emotions</u>. This helps the reader to <u>empathise</u> with him.

3) A <u>third-person</u> narrator is a separate voice, created by the author to tell the story — this type of narrator is used in 'A Christmas Carol' and 'Pride and Prejudice'. They usually describe the thoughts and feelings of several <u>different characters</u>, making them more of a <u>storyteller</u> than a <u>character</u>.

4) Third-person narrators can be <u>omniscient</u> (all-knowing) or <u>limited</u> (only aware of the thoughts and feelings of one character). They may also describe only what can be <u>seen</u> or <u>heard</u> — for example, in 'Animal Farm', the narrator usually just presents the reader with <u>factual information</u>.

Not all narrators are reliable

1) Don't automatically <u>trust</u> what a narrator says — they may be <u>unreliable</u>. This is particularly common with first-person narrators, who see things from their <u>own point of view</u>.

I have recorded in detail the events of my insignificant existence...

The first-person narrator of 'Jane Eyre' calls herself "<u>insignificant</u>", but the fact that she's the <u>main character</u> in the book suggests this <u>isn't true</u>.

2) Narrators are <u>not</u> the <u>same</u> person as the author, but watch out for examples of the writer's <u>viewpoint</u> being <u>revealed</u> through the narrator. For example:

Scrooge! a squeezing, wrenching, grasping, scraping, clutching, covetous old sinner!

The third-person narrator of 'A Christmas Carol' has <u>strong opinions</u> on Scrooge, which seem to be <u>Dickens's views</u>.

First-person narrators — would you Adam an' Eve it?

Novels have to have a narrator (someone's got to tell the story), but authors get to choose who the narrator is and how reliable they are. Always be aware of whose voice you're listening to and what the impact of that is.

19th-Century Fiction

You have to study a 19th-century novel, so these pages contain some useful background information on life in the period. This will help you understand the texts better, and to write more informed essays on them.

There was a big gap between the upper and lower classes

1) <u>Class</u> was <u>important</u> in the 19th century — your class <u>determined</u> what <u>kind</u> of life you had.

2) Early 19th-century society was divided between the <u>rich upper classes</u> (who <u>owned</u> the <u>land</u>, didn't need to <u>work</u> and so <u>socialised</u> a lot) and the <u>poorer working classes</u> (who <u>relied</u> on the upper classes for work, and were often <u>looked down on</u> because of it).

3) The <u>Industrial Revolution</u> created opportunities for more people to <u>make money</u>, meaning that the <u>middle classes</u> grew in <u>size</u> and <u>influence</u> throughout the century.

In the Industrial Revolution, technological advances meant that goods could be produced by machines in factories, rather than by hand in people's homes. This resulted in many people moving from working in farming (and living in the countryside) to working in manufacturing (and living in cities).

4) However, the fact that the <u>middle classes</u> relied on a <u>profession</u> or <u>trade</u> for their wealth meant that they were <u>looked down on</u> by the <u>upper classes</u>.

'Pride and Prejudice' examines and criticises judgements based on social status. Austen mocks 19th-century class prejudices by showing that characters' behaviour is down to personality, not class.

Many cities were overcrowded and had terrible living conditions

1) In the 19th century, millions of people moved from the countryside to the <u>cities</u> in search of <u>work</u> in the new factories. As a result, the <u>population</u> of cities grew rapidly and uncontrollably.

2) Most of these people ended up living in <u>slums</u> of cheap, overcrowded housing. There was often no proper drainage or <u>sewage</u> system, and many families had to share one tap and toilet. Overcrowding led to <u>hunger</u>, <u>disease</u> and <u>crime</u>.

Dickens uses 'A Christmas Carol' to highlight the problems and poverty of working-class London. He contrasts the wealth of Scrooge with the poverty of the Cratchit family.

Education wasn't compulsory until the late 19th century

1) Education was a <u>privilege</u> — only <u>wealthy</u> families could afford to send children away to school, or to hire a <u>governess</u> to live with them and teach the children.

2) Boys' education was more of a <u>priority</u>, and many girls weren't educated at all. An academic education was seen as <u>unnecessary</u> for women — girls from <u>rich</u> families were taught <u>art</u>, <u>music</u> and <u>dance</u> as this would help them to get a <u>husband</u>, and girls from <u>poorer</u> families were expected to go straight into a <u>job</u> that didn't require an <u>education</u>.

3) Many schools were run by the <u>Church</u> and supported by <u>charity donations</u>. The <u>government</u> began funding schools in <u>1833</u>, but the funding was very limited.

4) School <u>wasn't compulsory</u> until <u>1880</u>, when an Education Act finally made it compulsory for children between the ages of <u>five</u> and <u>ten</u> to attend school.

In 'Great Expectations', Pip receives hardly any formal education as a child. He is desperate to gain an education, believing this is key to becoming a gentleman, and attempts to improve his education throughout the novel.

Upon being given his new uniform, Jacob initially struggled to see the positives of compulsory education.

19th-Century Fiction

Women were often dependent on men

1) During the 19th century, women were normally dependent on the men in their family, especially in the upper classes. It was usually men who earned a living or owned land which generated income from rent.

2) A woman's best chance of a stable future was a good marriage — there were very few job options available for upper and middle-class women, and women often weren't allowed to inherit land or money.

3) Women didn't have the vote, and generally had to do what their husband told them — they were expected to stay at home and look after children.

> 'Jane Eyre' was unusual at the time of publication not only because it was written by a woman, but also because its main character is a determined and sometimes outspoken woman. By the end of the novel, Jane is both emotionally and financially independent.

Reputation was important

1) In middle and upper-class society, it was important to be respectable.

2) Christianity had a strong influence on standards of behaviour — people believed they should live by a strict moral code, which included attending church regularly, avoiding alcohol and exercising sexual restraint.

3) If someone was seen doing anything which wasn't considered respectable, their reputation could be ruined. To protect their reputation, people often kept their sinful behaviour and less respectable desires secret.

> The gentlemen in 'Dr Jekyll and Mr Hyde' are concerned with their reputations. Jekyll creates Hyde in order to hide his sins and preserve his reputation, and Utterson consistently tries to protect Jekyll's reputation. The book explores how this obsession with reputation can actually be destructive.

Many texts were influenced by Romanticism and the Gothic genre

1) 'Romanticism' had a big impact on literature and art in the late 18th century and the early 19th century.

2) The 'Romantics' tried to capture intense emotions and experiences in their work, and were especially influenced by nature. They saw nature as a powerful force that could inspire and restore people.

3) Many 19th-century writers were influenced by the Gothic genre — this generally involved a mysterious location, supernatural elements, troubling secrets and elements of madness.

4) The double (or doppelgänger) is another key feature of Gothic novels — it's where two characters are presented as if they are each a version of the other.

> 'Frankenstein' includes aspects of the 'Romantic' and the Gothic. Frankenstein travels to the Alps in the hope that the "magnificence" of nature will help him to forget his "sorrows", but it is there that he meets the monster, who is presented as the other side of him.

In summary — life in the 19th century was tough (unless you were rich and male...)

This isn't a history exam, so you don't have to know about the 19th century in detail... But, it's really important that you understand the context of the text you're reading, so you do need to learn these pages.

Poetry — What You Have To Do

Poetry is an important part of your English Literature GCSE. The next three sections will get you up to speed with what you need to do to write cracking poetry essays. Who knows, you might even end up enjoying it...

You'll write about poetry in at least one of your Literature exams

The poetry aspect of your GCSE English Literature course is divided into <u>two</u> main sections:

1) <u>Poetry anthology</u> (see Section Nine) — you'll study a group (or '<u>cluster</u>') of poems in class. The poems will share common themes.

2) <u>Unseen</u> poetry (see Section Ten) — in the exam, you have to write about one or more poems that you've never seen before. You'll get a copy of them in your exam paper and have to <u>analyse</u> them on the spot.

You could be asked about any poem from the group you've studied, so you need to know them all well.

You need to think about language, structure and form

For writing about language, see pages 55-57. For more on form and structure, see page 54.

You should always write about <u>language</u>, <u>structure</u> and <u>form</u> in your answers on poetry.

Language ⇨	This means looking at what <u>words</u> have been chosen and <u>why</u>. Consider any <u>imagery</u> and <u>poetic techniques</u> that've been used.
Structure ⇨	Structure is about the way a poem is put together. This includes how a poet arranges their <u>feelings</u> and <u>ideas</u> in a poem to convey them most <u>effectively</u>.
Form ⇨	Poems come in different <u>types</u> (or forms) e.g. a sonnet. Most forms have their own <u>rules</u> and <u>features</u> — they may have a set number of lines, or a fixed rhyme scheme.

You must show you appreciate what the poet is doing

1) Once you've identified points about language, structure and form, think about the <u>effects</u> that these features create.

2) To get the top marks, you need to consider what these effects <u>suggest</u> about the <u>speaker</u>, or how they <u>make</u> the <u>reader</u> feel.

3) You're the reader, so you should include your <u>personal opinion</u> — you can be as creative as you like, as long as you <u>back up</u> your idea with a <u>relevant quote</u> from the poem.

Geoffrey had many personal opinions about the poems... none of which he could put in the exam.

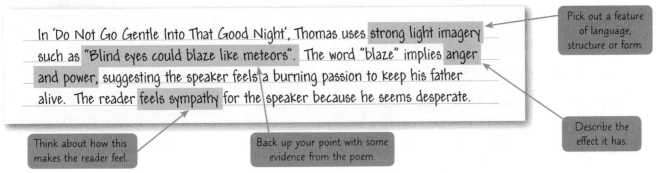

In 'Do Not Go Gentle Into That Good Night', Thomas uses strong light imagery such as "Blind eyes could blaze like meteors". The word "blaze" implies anger and power, suggesting the speaker feels a burning passion to keep his father alive. The reader feels sympathy for the speaker because he seems desperate.

Pick out a feature of language, structure or form.

Describe the effect it has.

Think about how this makes the reader feel.

Back up your point with some evidence from the poem.

The language, you say? — er, English, I think...

When reading a poem, don't get put off if you don't understand it right away. Go over it a couple of times and start to look at language, structure and form — they can often give you a clue about the poem's meaning.

Form and Structure

Form and structure are all about the way a poem is put together. Poets choose certain forms and structures for a reason — no, not to annoy you. (Well — maybe a bit.) Your job is to figure out what those reasons are.

Poetry comes in different forms

Different forms (or types) of poems follow different rules — that's how you can tell them apart. You need to be able to recognise different forms of poetry for your exam.

> Sometimes poets use a certain form but break some of its rules for effect.

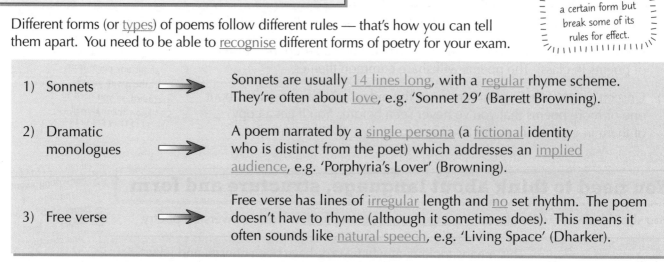

1) Sonnets ⟹ Sonnets are usually 14 lines long, with a regular rhyme scheme. They're often about love, e.g. 'Sonnet 29' (Barrett Browning).

2) Dramatic monologues ⟹ A poem narrated by a single persona (a fictional identity who is distinct from the poet) which addresses an implied audience, e.g. 'Porphyria's Lover' (Browning).

3) Free verse ⟹ Free verse has lines of irregular length and no set rhythm. The poem doesn't have to rhyme (although it sometimes does). This means it often sounds like natural speech, e.g. 'Living Space' (Dharker).

Learn the correct terms to describe form

To discuss form properly in the exam, you need to know and use the correct technical terms:

- A stanza (or verse) is a group of lines.

- A tercet is a three-line stanza.

- A quatrain is a four-line stanza.

- A couplet is a pair of lines, usually with the same metre (see p.55).

- A rhyming couplet is a couplet where the final words of each line rhyme.

- A rhyming triplet is where the final words of three successive lines rhyme with each other.

Structure is how a poem is arranged

Structure is how the poet arranges their feelings or ideas in a poem to convey them most effectively. Two poems with the same form can be structured very differently.

Think about:

The twins looked the same, but privately disagreed about their choice of hat.

1) How a poem begins and ends. See if the poet goes back to the same ideas, or if the poem progresses.

2) Any pauses or interruptions in ideas in the poem.

3) Changes in mood, voice, tense, rhyme scheme, rhythm or pace.

> Once you've identified a structural feature, you must always explain why you think the poet has used it.

Poems are like suitcases — you need to unpack them...

*Structure and form are really, **really**, **really** important — you have to discuss them in your exam. Don't just let language hog the limelight — if you forget about these fellas, you're missing out on crucial marks.*

Poetic Techniques

Rejoice happily, your teacher has marshmallows — there's no excuse for spelling 'rhythm' wrong in the exam.

Rhyme can add power to the poet's message

1) Rhyme helps a poem develop its beat or <u>rhythm</u>, but poets can also use it to reinforce the poem's <u>message</u>.

2) Rhyme can be <u>regular</u> (occurring in a set pattern), <u>irregular</u> (with no pattern) or <u>absent</u> from a poem.

3) This creates different <u>effects</u> — regular rhyme schemes can create a sense of <u>control</u>, whereas irregular rhyme schemes might show <u>chaos</u> or <u>unpredictability</u>. Often these effects link to the <u>themes</u> in a poem.

4) Sometimes rhymes occur within lines, too. These are called <u>internal rhymes</u>.

> In 'Neutral Tones' the ABBA rhyme scheme mirrors the cyclical structure of the poem — just as the poem begins and ends with the image of the pond, the 'A' rhyme returns at the end of each stanza. This reflects the way that the narrator's memory of the break-up returns to affect him.

Make sure you comment on the effect the rhyme scheme has, e.g. here it reinforces something about the narrator.

Rhythm alters the pace and mood of a poem

1) Rhythm is the <u>arrangement</u> of beats within a line. It's easier to <u>feel</u> a rhythm than to see it on the page.

2) Like rhyme, rhythm can be <u>regular</u> or <u>irregular</u>. A <u>strong</u> rhyme scheme often creates a <u>regular</u> rhythm.

3) Rhythm can affect the <u>pace</u> (speed) and <u>mood</u> of a poem — a fast rhythm can make a poem seem <u>rushed</u> and <u>frantic</u>, whereas a slow and regular rhythm can make a poem seem <u>calm</u>.

4) Sometimes poets use rhythm to <u>imitate</u> sounds related to the poem, e.g. a heartbeat or beating drums.

> In 'The Farmer's Bride', Mew uses monosyllabic words in the final stanza, e.g. "Oh! my God!", to break down the rhythm. This draws attention to the farmer's loss of self-control.

When talking about a change in rhythm, don't forget to describe what the change is and the significance of it.

Metre is the pattern of syllables in a line

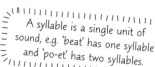

A syllable is a single unit of sound, e.g. 'beat' has one syllable and 'po-et' has two syllables.

1) In poetry, the rhythm of a line is created by <u>patterns</u> of <u>syllables</u>. If the patterns are <u>consistent</u>, then the poem's rhythm is <u>regular</u>.

2) <u>Metre</u> is the technical term for these patterns. There are different types of metre, depending on which syllables are <u>stressed</u> (emphasised) and which are <u>unstressed</u>.

<u>Iambic pentameter</u> is a metre that's commonly used in poetry. It has 10 syllables in a line — an <u>unstressed</u> syllable followed by a <u>stressed</u> syllable, repeated five times over.

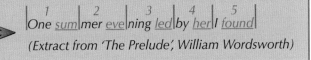

(Extract from 'The Prelude', William Wordsworth)

All this talk of syllables is stressing me out...

Welcome to the nitty gritty technical stuff. It's a lot to get your head around, but it does look impressive if you can write about rhyme and rhythm in the exam — practise analysing them in your anthology poems.

Poetic Techniques

Imagery is when a poet uses language to create a picture. The key to analysing imagery is to always ask yourself why that image has been chosen. (And then try to come up with an answer.)

Similes and metaphors add power to descriptions

1) Similes <u>compare</u> one thing to another — they often contain the words '<u>like</u>' or '<u>as</u>'.

2) Similes are frequently used to <u>exaggerate</u> — the poet usually wants to <u>emphasise</u> something.

> "<u>like</u> a satellite
> *Wrenched from its orbit, go drifting away*"
> *('Walking Away' — C. Day Lewis)*

→ The narrator uses the simile of a "<u>satellite</u>" that is "<u>Wrenched from its orbit</u>" to describe his son walking away — this creates a vivid image of an object <u>lost</u> in space, emphasising the father's <u>anxiety</u>.

3) Metaphors describe something as though it <u>is</u> something else.

4) They take an object or person and give it the <u>qualities</u> of something else. This means that the poet can put a lot of <u>meaning</u> into a few words.

An extended metaphor is when a poet uses several metaphors which explore the same idea, theme or topic.

> "the <u>foetus of metal</u> beneath his chest"
> *('The Manhunt' — Simon Armitage)*

→ The narrator uses the metaphor "<u>the foetus of metal</u>" to describe the bullet in her partner's chest — this makes the bullet seem like an active part of the man, suggesting that he is <u>still living</u> with its effects.

Personification gives an object human qualities

1) Personification means describing an <u>object</u> as if it feels or behaves in a <u>human way</u>.

2) It can add <u>emotion</u> or alter the <u>mood</u> of a poem — this can really help the poet convey their <u>message</u>.

> "The <u>sullen</u> wind was soon <u>awake</u>"
> *('Porphyria's Lover' — Robert Browning)*

→ Browning personifies the wind as "<u>sullen</u>", stating it was "<u>soon awake</u>". This sets a <u>threatening mood</u>, as the bad-tempered wind has been disturbed.

Imagery isn't just visual

1) Poets often appeal to all the senses (touch, sight, sound, smell and taste) — this is called <u>sensory imagery</u>.

2) Sensory imagery helps to create a <u>vivid image</u> in the reader's mind.

"Ahh sensory imagery, not sensual imagery — no wonder I got that detention..."

> "the skin of his finger is <u>smooth</u> and <u>thick</u>
> like <u>warm ice</u>."
> *('Climbing My Grandfather' — Andrew Waterhouse)*

→ Waterhouse uses sensory imagery such as "smooth", "thick" and "like warm ice" to show the <u>close bond</u> between the narrator and their grandfather.

This revision guide is your passport to prosperity... (vomit)

Most of these techniques are pretty easy to spot once you've understood them — good thing too, because poems are crammed full of them. They'll give you loads of stuff to talk about in the exam, so get learning.

Poetic Techniques

Being able to identify poetic techniques correctly and commenting on their effect will mean marks heading your way. Using the correct terms for the techniques is the icing on that exam-shaped cake.

Poets use the sounds of words for effect

The sounds words create can alter the <u>mood</u>, <u>pace</u> and <u>tone</u> of a poem. Here are some of the most common <u>techniques</u> that use sound for effect:

> Mood is the atmosphere of a poem, and tone is the feeling the words are spoken with.

1) <u>Alliteration</u> is where words that are close together <u>start</u> with the <u>same sound</u>.

| *"me with my <u>h</u>eartful of <u>h</u>eadlines"*
 ('Letters from Yorkshire' — Maura Dooley) | ➡ | The repeated 'h' sound creates a sense of <u>heaviness</u>, which reflects the narrator's <u>discontent</u> with her life. |

2) <u>Assonance</u> is when <u>vowel</u> sounds are <u>repeated</u>.

| *"How should I gr<u>ee</u>t th<u>ee</u>?"*
 ('When We Two Parted' — Lord Byron) | ➡ | The <u>assonant long</u> 'ee' sounds <u>draw out</u> each word — this reflects the <u>long-lasting</u> nature of the narrator's <u>pain</u>. |

3) <u>Sibilance</u> is when sounds create a '<u>hissing</u>' or '<u>shushing</u>' effect.

| *"My mother <u>sh</u>ade<u>s</u> her eye<u>s</u> and look<u>s</u> my way"*
 ('Eden Rock' — Charles Causley) | ➡ | The '<u>s</u>' and '<u>sh</u>' sounds create a <u>hushed tone</u>, reflecting the <u>tranquillity</u> of the scene. |

4) <u>Onomatopoeia</u> is when a word <u>mimics</u> the sound it's describing.

| *"To get out of that blue <u>crackling</u> air"*
 ('Bayonet Charge' — Ted Hughes) | ➡ | "Crackling" makes the air sound <u>electric</u> and <u>fragile</u>, emphasising the <u>immediacy of danger</u> on the battlefield. |

Punctuation affects how a poem flows

Punctuation can affect the <u>pace</u> of a poem, emphasise <u>specific words</u>, or <u>interrupt</u> a poem's <u>rhythm</u>.

1) When punctuation creates a <u>pause</u> during a line of poetry, this is called a <u>caesura</u>.

| *"Happy and proud<u>;</u> at last I knew*
 Porphyria worshipped me<u>;</u> surprise"
 ('Porphyria's Lover' — Robert Browning) | ➡ | The semicolons create <u>caesurae</u> which make the poem sound <u>fragmented</u>, reflecting the narrator's <u>unstable mind</u>. |

2) <u>Enjambment</u> is when a <u>sentence</u> or <u>phrase</u> runs over from <u>one line</u> of poetry into the <u>next one</u>. Often enjambment puts emphasis on the <u>last word</u> of the first line or on the <u>first word</u> of the next line.

| *"All I ever did was <u>follow</u>*
 In his broad shadow"
 ('Follower' — Seamus Heaney) | ➡ | The <u>enjambment</u> puts stress on the <u>final word</u> of the first line, emphasising the way the narrator trails behind his father. |

3) An <u>end-stopped line</u> is a line of poetry that ends in a <u>definite pause</u>, usually created by <u>punctuation</u>. End-stopped lines can help to maintain a <u>regular rhythm</u> and can also affect the <u>pace</u> of a poem.

I've had enough of this, full stop...

Learning these techniques is really important — the more you can recognise, the more you'll have to talk about in the exam. Plus, using the correct technical terms will earn you marks from the examiner.

Comparing Poems

In the exam you'll have to compare two poems — they could be seen or unseen. Here are some general tips...

Compare both poems in every paragraph

1) When you're asked to compare poems, you need to find <u>similarities</u> and <u>differences</u> between them.

2) This means you need to discuss <u>both poems</u> in <u>every paragraph</u>. There's a lot to squeeze in, so it's important to <u>structure</u> your paragraphs well.

3) <u>Comparative words</u> help you to do this. They clearly show the examiner if the point you're making is a <u>similarity</u> or <u>difference</u> between the two poems. Here are some useful examples:

Similarly...	*...also...*		*By contrast...*	*Unlike...*	*Conversely...*
Likewise...	*In the same way...*		*On the other hand...*	*However...*	*...yet...*
Equally...	*Both...*		*...whereas...*	*In comparison...*	*...but...*

Compare language, structure and form

When you plan your answer, make sure you consider <u>language</u>, <u>structure</u> and <u>form</u> — that way you won't forget to write about them in your essay.

Planning your work is essential for writing a top essay — there's a sample plan for a poetry comparison on p.64 to help you out.

Language

- Think about the <u>language techniques</u> the poets have used, e.g. <u>rhyme</u>, <u>imagery</u>, <u>sound</u>.

- Comment on how the language used in each poem is <u>similar</u> or <u>different</u>, and explain <u>why</u>.

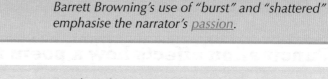 *Both 'Before You Were Mine' and 'Sonnet 29' use <u>onomatopoeia</u> to emphasise <u>strong emotions</u>. Duffy's verb "stamping" reflects the mother's <u>frustration</u> about her loss of freedom. Similarly, Barrett Browning's use of "burst" and "shattered" emphasise the narrator's <u>passion</u>.*

Structure

- Compare the <u>beginnings</u> and <u>endings</u> of the poems, and how the ideas and feelings presented are developed.

- Comment on changes in <u>mood</u>, <u>voice</u>, <u>tense</u> and <u>tone</u> — think about <u>the effect</u> this has.

In 'London', the narrative <u>begins</u> and <u>ends</u> on the dismal streets of London, suggesting that its inhabitants are <u>unable to escape</u> the suffering found there. In contrast, 'War Photographer' <u>ends</u> in a different place to where it <u>begins</u>. However, the fact that the photographer is starting another assignment highlights the <u>unending cycle</u> of war and violence.

Form

- See if the poems have a certain <u>form</u> and explain <u>why</u> you think the poet has made that choice.

- Compare the <u>effects</u> of form in each poem. Think about how they relate to the <u>themes</u>.

- Check if any rules are broken for <u>effect</u>, e.g. a sonnet with 15 lines instead of 14.

 'Sonnet 43' is a <u>sonnet</u>. By choosing a form traditionally used for love poems, Barrett Browning stresses <u>the strength of the love</u> between the narrator and her beloved. On the other hand, 'Living Space' is written in <u>free verse</u> — the <u>irregular line lengths</u> defy constraint, which echoes the <u>uncontrollable force of poverty</u>.

I compared her to a summer's day — then she slapped me...

Comparison essays can be a bit tricky, but as long as you remember to discuss the language, structure and form of both poems in the exam, then you should be fine (provided you also remember your pen).

The Poetry Anthology

If you're doing English Literature, you'll study a collection of poems in class and write about them in the exam. This section tells you how to write a cracking answer that'll help you on your way to a top grade.

This is what you'll have to do in the exam

1) You'll probably be given a copy of <u>one poem</u> from your anthology, and asked to compare it with <u>another</u> poem of your <u>choice</u>. You need to choose a poem that has <u>similar themes</u> to the one you're given.

2) You <u>won't</u> have a copy of the anthology in the exam, so make sure you know <u>all</u> the poems really well.

For some exam boards, you might be asked to compare a poem from your anthology with a poem you haven't seen before — see Section Ten for more on how to tackle unseen poetry. Ask your teacher exactly what to expect in the exam.

Read the question carefully and underline key words

1) If your exam board offers <u>more than one</u> poetry cluster, make sure you're looking at the <u>right one</u>. Read the question carefully. Underline the <u>theme</u> and any other <u>key words</u>.

2) Here are a couple of examples of the kind of <u>question</u> you might get in the exam:

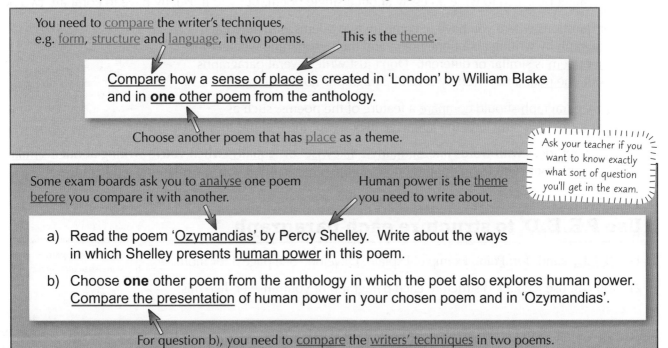

You need to <u>compare</u> the writer's techniques, e.g. <u>form</u>, <u>structure</u> and <u>language</u>, in two poems.   This is the <u>theme</u>.

Compare how a <u>sense of place</u> is created in 'London' by William Blake and in **one** other poem from the anthology.

Choose another poem that has <u>place</u> as a theme.

Some exam boards ask you to <u>analyse</u> one poem <u>before</u> you compare it with another.   Human power is the <u>theme</u> you need to write about.

Ask your teacher if you want to know exactly what sort of question you'll get in the exam.

a) Read the poem '<u>Ozymandias</u>' by Percy Shelley. Write about the ways in which Shelley presents <u>human power</u> in this poem.

b) Choose **one** other poem from the anthology in which the poet also explores human power. <u>Compare the presentation</u> of human power in your chosen poem and in 'Ozymandias'.

For question b), you need to <u>compare</u> the <u>writers' techniques</u> in two poems.

There are three main ways to get marks

There are <u>three main things</u> to keep in mind when you're <u>planning</u> and <u>writing</u> your answer:

- Give your own <u>thoughts</u> and <u>opinions</u> on the poems and support them with <u>quotes</u> from the text.
- <u>Explain</u> features like <u>form</u>, <u>structure</u> and <u>language</u>.
- Describe the <u>similarities</u> and <u>differences</u> between poems and their <u>contexts</u>.

How do I love poetry? Let me count the ways...

At the risk of sounding like a broken record, it's crucial that you know the poems really well for the exam — learn some key quotes from each one that you can include in your answer to back up your points.

How to Structure Your Answer

A solid structure is essential — it lets the examiner follow your argument nice and easily. The best way to make sure you write a well-structured essay in the exam is to make a plan before you start writing (see p.2).

Start with an introduction and end with a conclusion

1) Your introduction should begin by giving a clear answer to the question in a sentence or two. Use the rest of the introduction to briefly develop this idea — try to include some of the main ideas from your plan.

2) The main body of your essay should be three to five paragraphs of analysis.

3) Finish your essay with a conclusion — this should summarise your answer to the question. It's also your last chance to impress the examiner, so try to make your final sentence memorable.

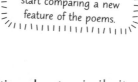

The examiner found Sam's final sentence memorable for all the wrong reasons.

© iStockphoto.com/AndreyPopov

You'll probably have to compare two poems

1) You might be asked to write an essay about a single poem, but you'll usually have to compare two poems.

2) For questions where you have to compare two poems, structure each paragraph by writing about one poem and then explaining whether the other poem is similar or different. Don't just write several paragraphs about one poem, followed by several paragraphs about the other.

Remember to start a new paragraph every time you start comparing a new feature of the poems.

3) Every paragraph should compare a feature of the poems, such as their form, their structure, the language they use or the feelings they put across.

4) Link your ideas with words like 'similarly', 'likewise' or 'equally' when you're writing about a similarity. Or use phrases such as 'in contrast' and 'on the other hand' if you're explaining a difference.

Use P.E.E.D. to structure each paragraph

This extract shows how to use P.E.E.D. in a comparison essay, but the same structure applies if you're writing about a single poem.

1) P.E.E.D. stands for: Point, Example, Explain, Develop. See page 3 for more.

2) You can use P.E.E.D to structure each paragraph of your answer, like this:

Start with a point that compares the two poems.

Give examples from both poems.

'The Charge of the Light Brigade' and 'Bayonet Charge' both emphasise the sounds of battle. Tennyson repeats the onomatopoeic verbs "Volley'd", "thunder'd" and "Storm'd" to suggest the noise of the cannons that the Light Brigade faced. Similarly, in 'Bayonet Charge', the metaphor "blue crackling air" uses onomatopoeia to vividly depict the noise of machine gun fire. In both poems, this emphasis on sound adds a horrifying dimension to the depictions of conflict, making them vivid and realistic for the reader.

Explain how the examples relate to your opening point.

Sometimes you can develop your point for both poems at the same time.

I've got better at introductions since I joined that dating website...

P.E.E.D. is just a framework to make sure your paragraphs have all the features they need to pick up marks — it's a useful structure to bear in mind, but you don't have to follow it rigidly in every paragraph.

How to Answer the Question

The exam is no time to discover your inner politician — you actually need to answer the question you're given.

Look closely at language, form and structure

1) To get <u>top marks</u>, you need to pay <u>close attention</u> to the <u>techniques</u> the poets use.

2) <u>Analyse</u> the <u>form</u> and <u>structure</u> of the poems, which includes their <u>rhyme scheme</u> and <u>rhythm</u>.

3) Explore <u>language</u> — think about <u>why</u> the poets have used certain <u>words</u> and <u>language techniques</u>.

4) You also need to <u>comment</u> on the <u>effect</u> that these techniques have on the <u>reader</u>. The examiner wants to hear what <u>you think</u> of a poem and how it makes <u>you feel</u>.

5) This is the kind of thing you could write about <u>language</u>:

> 'Poppies' makes frequent references to the injury and bereavement caused by conflict. The poem opens with a reference to the poppies placed "on individual war graves". By emphasising the personal, individual loss that conflict can cause, Weir highlights the narrator's fear that her own son will be killed in battle. The narrator's anxiety about the violence of conflict is further suggested by the depiction of poppy petals as "spasms of paper red". This metaphor evokes a vivid image of the physical injury that the narrator fears her son may suffer as a soldier, which helps the reader to understand the narrator's fears and to empathise with her.

Analyse the effects of key quotes.

Always develop your ideas.

Always support your ideas with details from the text

1) To get <u>top marks</u>, you need to <u>back up your ideas</u> with <u>quotes</u> from or <u>references</u> to the text.

2) <u>Choose</u> your quotes <u>carefully</u> — they have to be <u>relevant</u> to the point you're making.

3) <u>Don't</u> quote <u>large chunks</u> of text — instead, use <u>short</u> quotes and <u>embed</u> them in your sentences.

> ✘ In 'Sonnet 43', the narrator shows how much she loves her partner — "I love thee to the depth and breadth and height / My soul can reach, when feeling out of sight".

This quote is too long and it doesn't fit into the sentence structure.

> ✓ The narrator emphasises the strength of her love by referring to its "depth and breadth and height", highlighting that it extends as far as her "soul can reach".

These quotes are nicely embedded into the sentence.

4) <u>Don't</u> forget to <u>explain</u> your quotes — you need to use them as <u>evidence</u> to support your <u>argument</u>.

This just describes what happens in the poem.

> ✘ In 'The Prelude', Wordsworth shows that nature can be frightening. The narrator sees "a huge peak" that "Upreared its head" and "Strode after" him.

This explains how the quotes support the argument.

> ✓ Wordsworth presents nature as a frightening presence. The phrase "Upreared its head" makes the "huge peak" seem monstrous, and its calm pursuit of the narrator adds menace.

How to Answer the Question

Give alternative interpretations

1) You need to show you're aware that poems can be <u>interpreted</u> in <u>more than one</u> way.

2) If a poem is a bit <u>ambiguous</u>, or you think that a particular line or phrase could have several <u>different meanings</u>, then <u>say so</u>.

Remember to support your interpretations with evidence from the poem.

> In 'Ozymandias', Shelley refers to the sculptor as the "hand that mocked" the statue. On the surface, the word "mocked" shows only that the sculptor created the artwork. However, Shelley may also be playing on the second meaning of the word "mocked" (to make fun of); the "wrinkled lip and sneer" of the statue suggest that the sculptor disliked Ozymandias, hinting that he may have intended to ridicule the leader by his unflattering depiction.

3) Be <u>original</u> with your ideas — just make sure you can back them up with an <u>example</u> from the text.

Show some wider knowledge

1) To get a top grade, you need to <u>explain</u> how the <u>ideas</u> in the poems relate to their <u>context</u>.

2) When you're thinking about a particular poem, consider these aspects of <u>context</u>:

Historical — Do the ideas in the poem relate to the <u>time</u> in which it's <u>written</u> or <u>set</u>?

Geographical — How is the poem shaped and influenced by the <u>place</u> in which it's set?

Social — Is the poet <u>criticising</u> or <u>praising</u> the <u>society</u> or <u>community</u> they're writing about?

Cultural — Does the poet draw on a particular aspect of their <u>background</u> or <u>culture</u>?

Literary — Was the poet influenced by other <u>works of literature</u> or a particular <u>literary movement</u>?

3) Here are a couple of <u>examples</u> of how you might use <u>context</u> in your <u>answer</u>:

> In 'London', Blake's reference to the "chimney-sweeper's cry" creates a vivid picture of child labour, which was common in the late 18th century. Blake considered child labour to be morally wrong, and he may have included this emotive image in order to boost public sympathy for his views.

> Browning is thought to have based the speaker in 'My Last Duchess' on the Duke of Ferrara, an important nobleman in Renaissance Italy. The Italian Renaissance was a time of great artistic innovation, but it was also infamous for its violence and bloodshed. These dual aspects of society are reflected in the Duke's pride in his art collection and in his apparent lack of guilt about seemingly having had his wife killed.

How to Answer the Question

Use sophisticated language

1) Your writing has to sound <u>sophisticated</u> and <u>precise</u>.

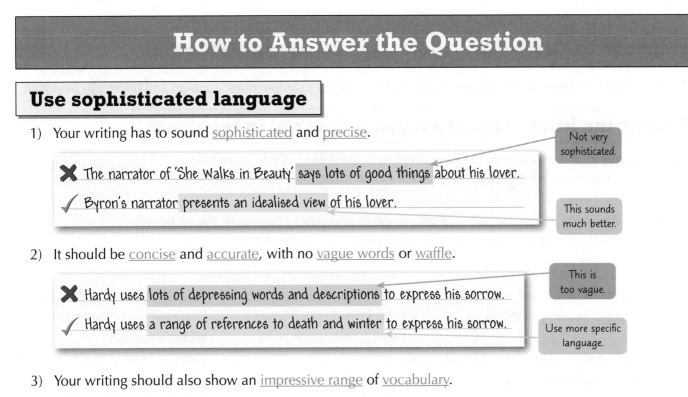

✗ The narrator of 'She Walks in Beauty' says lots of good things about his lover. — Not very sophisticated.

✓ Byron's narrator presents an idealised view of his lover. — This sounds much better.

2) It should be <u>concise</u> and <u>accurate</u>, with no <u>vague words</u> or <u>waffle</u>.

✗ Hardy uses lots of depressing words and descriptions to express his sorrow. — This is too vague.

✓ Hardy uses a range of references to death and winter to express his sorrow. — Use more specific language.

3) Your writing should also show an <u>impressive range</u> of <u>vocabulary</u>.

Don't keep using the same word to describe something.

✗ In 'Poppies', the narrator feels cut off from her son. The word "blockade" shows that she feels cut off from him. The idea that she feels cut off from her son is also shown by the description of his hair as "gelled blackthorns".

Vary how you say things — it sounds much more impressive.

✓ In 'Poppies', the narrator feels cut off from her son. This sense of separation is emphasised by the metaphor describing his hair as "gelled blackthorns", which suggests that her son has become prickly and unapproachable.

4) However, make sure you <u>only</u> use words that you know the <u>meaning</u> of. For example, don't say that a poem has a '<u>volta</u>' if you don't know what it <u>really means</u> — it will be <u>obvious</u> to the examiner.

Use technical terms where possible

1) To get top marks, you need to use the <u>correct technical terms</u> when you're writing about poetry.

2) Flick back to Section Eight for more on these terms, or have a look at the <u>glossary</u> at the back of the book.

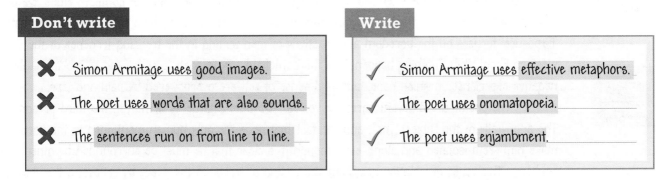

Don't write

✗ Simon Armitage uses good images.

✗ The poet uses words that are also sounds.

✗ The sentences run on from line to line.

Write

✓ Simon Armitage uses effective metaphors.

✓ The poet uses onomatopoeia.

✓ The poet uses enjambment.

My mother always told me that rhyme doesn't pay...

... at least, I think that's what she said. So I gave up my dream of being a poet and started writing revision guides instead. On the downside, very little of my work rhymes. On the upside, I can write as many puns as I want.

Section Nine — English Literature: Poetry Anthology

Sample Answer

Writing essays on the poetry anthology can be tricky, so here's a sample question, plan and answer to help you.

This is the kind of question you might get in the exam

The <u>exam question</u> for the poetry anthology will look something like the one below. Spend five minutes drawing up a <u>plan</u> — it's the key to a <u>well-structured</u> essay.

Have a look at pages 2-4 for tips on how to plan and write English essays.

> Read 'Bayonet Charge' by Ted Hughes. Choose one other poem from the anthology and compare how the reality of conflict is presented in the two poems.

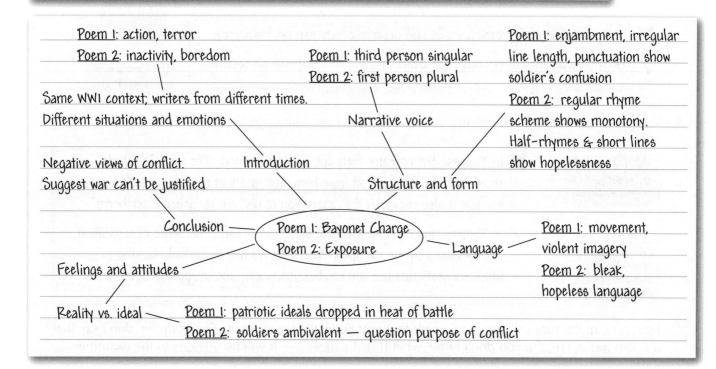

Poem 1: action, terror
Poem 2: inactivity, boredom

Same WWI context; writers from different times.
Different situations and emotions

Negative views of conflict.
Suggest war can't be justified

Introduction

Conclusion

Feelings and attitudes

Reality vs. ideal

Poem 1: third person singular
Poem 2: first person plural

Narrative voice

Structure and form

Poem 1: Bayonet Charge
Poem 2: Exposure

Language

Poem 1: patriotic ideals dropped in heat of battle
Poem 2: soldiers ambivalent — question purpose of conflict

Poem 1: enjambment, irregular line length, punctuation show soldier's confusion
Poem 2: regular rhyme scheme shows monotony. Half-rhymes & short lines show hopelessness

Poem 1: movement, violent imagery
Poem 2: bleak, hopeless language

This is how you could use the plan to write a really good answer

Compare the poems in your opening sentence.

Sum up the main argument of your essay.

Try to develop your ideas.

Although the action of both 'Bayonet Charge' and 'Exposure' occurs on the battlefields of World War One, the poems offer two very different portrayals of the reality of conflict. While 'Bayonet Charge' depicts the violent action and overwhelming terror experienced by a soldier going into battle, 'Exposure' focuses on the boredom and inactivity of men waiting in the freezing trenches of the Western Front while "nothing happens" on the battlefield. Both poets present war as a profoundly negative experience, in which hope, faith and sense of self are overpowered by pain and fear.

The poems use different narrative voices. 'Bayonet Charge' is written in the third person. The anonymity of the subject, "he", and the fact that he is the only human mentioned in the poem make him seem isolated and alone, even though it is clear that he must be surrounded by other soldiers. This sense of isolation heightens the feeling of terror in the poem by reflecting the soldier's acute focus on his own survival. In contrast, 'Exposure' is written in the first person plural ("our memory", "we hear"), which creates a sense of the shared suffering experienced by the millions of soldiers who fought and died in the First World War. This emphasises the vast scale of misery and loss of life in the war.

Sample Answer

The poets also use other aspects of form and structure to present the reality of conflict. In 'Bayonet Charge', Hughes uses enjambment and uneven line lengths to create an irregular rhythm, echoing the confusion experienced by the soldier. The irregular rhythm is heightened by caesurae in lines 11 and 15. These help to turn the second stanza into a pause in the action, which reflects the soldier's experience of time apparently standing still as he struggles to understand "the reason / Of his still running". In contrast, Owen uses a regular rhyme scheme (ABBAC) to emphasise the monotony experienced by the soldiers. Despite this regularity, half-rhymes such as "wire" / "war" create a sense of jarring discomfort that mirrors the soldiers' suffering.

The different experiences of conflict presented in 'Exposure' and 'Bayonet Charge' are conveyed through the contrasting language the poets use. Owen's language is bleak and hopeless — dawn is personified as a "melancholy army" "massing in the east", a metaphor which has a powerful effect on the reader by subverting their expectations — dawn is usually a symbol of hope, but here it only brings more "poignant misery". The soldiers' sense of hopelessness is also evident in the phrase "love of God seems dying", which suggests that the horrific reality of conflict is causing them to lose their faith in God, or perhaps to believe that a God who can subject them to such suffering has lost faith in them. In contrast to this bleak imagery, 'Bayonet Charge' is filled with frantic movement. Active verbs such as "running", "stumbling" and "plunged" help to create a vivid image of the soldier's desperate actions as he races into battle. The sense of movement in the poem is also conveyed by the opening phrase, "Suddenly he awoke", which places the reader in the middle of the action from the start. This phrase gives the poem a nightmarish quality, highlighting the feelings of confusion and terror that are driving the soldier.

Both poems suggest that the reality of conflict does not match up to the ideal. In 'Bayonet Charge', Hughes questions the patriotic ideals of "King, honour, human dignity, etcetera", arguing that in the heat of battle they are "Dropped like luxuries" as terror takes over. Information about the horrors of World War One was readily available in the 1950s when Hughes wrote this poem, and there is a sense of pity for the soldiers who fought. Similarly, in 'Exposure', the narrator questions whether anything is achieved by the soldiers' sacrifice. On the surface, the phrase "Since we believe not otherwise can kind fires burn" suggests the soldiers believe their sacrifice is necessary to protect the "kind fires" of home, but the complex, broken syntax reflects their lack of conviction that this is true. This reveals the sense of alienation many soldiers felt: they believed no-one at home appreciated their sacrifice.

'Bayonet Charge' and 'Exposure' both present vividly negative views of the reality of conflict for soldiers on the front line. The experience of the soldiers in the two poems is very different: Hughes focuses on the raw terror and active suffering of a soldier going into battle, whereas Owen concentrates on the hopelessness and passive suffering of men dying from exposure. However, both poets use structure, form and vivid imagery to powerfully convey the soldiers' suffering. Both narrators question the patriotic ideals used to justify war, suggesting instead that there can be no justification for the bleak and dehumanising reality of conflict.

Compare the poems' form and structure.

Use the correct technical terms.

Compare the language used in the two poems.

Suggest more than one interpretation of the poem.

Use quotes to support your argument.

Explain the effect of the examples you give.

Bring in some contextual details to your answer.

Your last sentence should sum up your argument, and it needs to be memorable.

Well, that was depressing...

Of course, you might be lucky enough to be studying a poetry anthology on a cheery topic, such as love and relationships. And that most definitely won't involve any heartbreak, pain or misery. Oh no.

How to Write a Top Grade Answer

Ahhh, grade 9, the Holy Grail that we've all been aspiring to (at least since we stopped hankering after an A*). There's no single way to get a grade 9 in the poetry exam, but here are a few tips to help you on your way...

Know the poems inside out

You have to know the poems, their key themes and techniques like the back of your hand. Everyone has their own ways of understanding poetry, but here are a few ideas of how to get to grips with them:

- Read the poems again and again, highlight bits, jot down notes — whatever works for you.
- Make a list of the key themes, and note down plenty of quotes that relate to each one.
- List the major techniques that the poet uses, along with the effect they have.

Memorise your lists in time for the exam.

Be as original as you can

1) There are no wrong interpretations of a poem, so come up with your own ideas.

2) Make sure you can back up your interpretations with evidence from the text. For example:

> In 'The Manhunt', Armitage's narrator describes the soldier's scar as a "frozen river". This creates a vivid image of a river eroding a land surface, emphasising the depth of the injury and the power of the object that harmed him. The fact that the scar is "frozen" implies that, for the moment at least, no more damage is being done.

Write about the poems critically

1) Being critical means giving your own opinions about the poems — e.g. how effective you think the poet's techniques are, and why you think this.

2) You need to phrase your opinions in a sophisticated way. For example:

> In 'Neutral Tones', the phrase "God-curst sun" compels the reader to experience the scene as Hardy's narrator does: a bleak, lifeless landscape, devoid of hope and forsaken by God.

Get to grips with context

It's not enough just to mention a link to context — you need to really explore the effect it has on the poem, or on your understanding of it. For example:

© iStockphoto.com/Ljupco

> In common with other Romantic poets, Wordsworth viewed nature as a powerful force that could inspire and transform people. This is evident in the extract from his autobiographical poem 'The Prelude'; the encounter with the "huge peak" leaves him in a "grave / And serious mood", seemingly forcing him to contemplate his own mortality and place in the Universe.

Colin hoped the transformation would happen soon — his arm was getting tired.

Grade 9 — for the ninjas of the GCSE English world...

*I've got two bits of exciting news — that's the end of this section, and the next section is about unseen poetry. I don't know about you, but I can't wait to find out how you're supposed to write about invisible poetry.**

* It's possible that I've misunderstood this bit of the exam.

Five Steps to Analysing a Poem

You'll have to analyse unseen poetry at some point in your English Literature exams — here's how to do it.

The examiner is looking for four main things

You'll usually be asked to answer a question on an <u>unseen poem</u>, and then <u>compare</u> it with another poem.

To impress the examiner, you need to:

1) Show that you <u>understand</u> what the poems are <u>about</u>.

2) Write about the <u>techniques</u> used in the poems.

3) Use the <u>correct technical terms</u> to describe the techniques in the poems.

4) <u>Support</u> every point you make with <u>quotes</u> or <u>examples</u> from the poems.

After an extensive search for supporting evidence, Barry was forced to admit that his point might be flawed.

Five steps to analysing an unseen poem

Pick out the important bits of the poem as you read it — underline them or make notes.

1) Work out what the poem's about

- Work out the <u>subject</u> of the poem, e.g. the poem is about the narrator's relationship with his parents.
- Think about <u>who</u> is <u>speaking</u>, and <u>who</u> the poem is <u>addressing</u> — e.g. the narrator's lover, the reader...

2) Identify the purpose, theme or message

- Think about <u>what</u> the poet is saying, <u>why</u> they've written the poem, or what <u>ideas</u> they're using.
- The poem could be an <u>emotional response</u> to something. It might aim to <u>get a response</u> from the <u>reader</u>, or put across a message or an opinion about something.

3) Explore the emotions, moods or feelings

- Consider the <u>different emotions or feelings</u> in the poem and identify its <u>mood</u>.
- Look at how the poet <u>shows</u> these emotions (see step 4).

4) Identify the techniques used in the poem

- Find the <u>different techniques</u> (see p.54-57) the poet has used and how they create <u>emotions</u>, <u>moods</u> or <u>feelings</u>. Think about <u>why</u> the poet has used them, and what <u>effect</u> they create.
- Techniques can be related to <u>language</u> (<u>alliteration</u>, <u>onomatopoeia</u>, <u>imagery</u> etc.), <u>structure</u> (the order of <u>ideas</u> and any changes in <u>mood</u> or <u>tone</u>) and <u>form</u> (<u>line</u> and <u>stanza</u> length, <u>rhyme schemes</u> etc.).

5) Include your thoughts and feelings about the poem

- Examiners love to hear what <u>you think</u> of a poem and how it makes <u>you feel</u>. Think about how well the poem gets its <u>message</u> across and what <u>impact</u> it has on you.
- Try <u>not</u> to use "<u>I</u>" though — don't say "I felt sad that the narrator's brother died", it's much <u>better</u> to say "It makes the reader feel the narrator's sense of sadness at the death of his brother."
- Think about any <u>other ways</u> that the poem could be <u>interpreted</u>.

Step one — reveal any invisible ink...

These five steps will save your bacon in the exam, so learn them well. Don't forget that one poem can have loads of different themes, messages and ideas squeezed into just a few lines — there should be tons to say.

Analysing a Poem

The first thing to do when you're analysing a poem is read the question carefully and underline the key words.

Make sure you understand the question

It's asking 'what's the poem's message about death and the afterlife?'

In 'His Visitor', how does the poet present death and the afterlife?

The question wants you to write about what techniques the poet uses, e.g. form, structure and language.

This is how you might annotate a poem

Read through the poem and mark any bits of it that stand out. Then jot down your thoughts on each one.

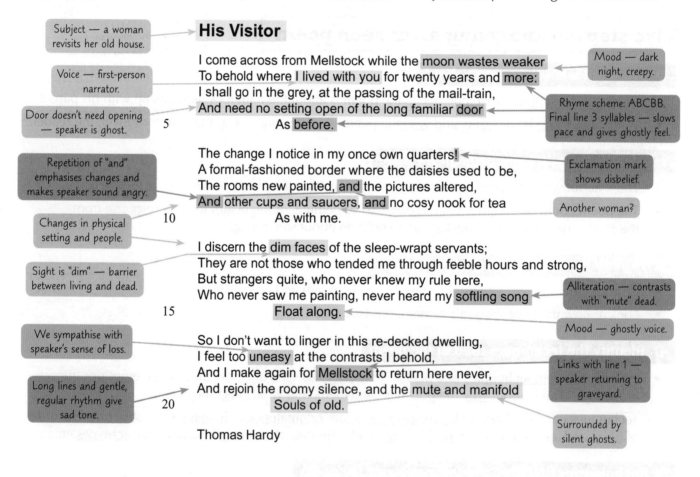

His Visitor

Subject — a woman revisits her old house.

Voice — first-person narrator.

Door doesn't need opening — speaker is ghost.

I come across from Mellstock while the moon wastes weaker
To behold where I lived with you for twenty years and more:
I shall go in the grey, at the passing of the mail-train,
And need no setting open of the long familiar door
     As before.

5

Mood — dark night, creepy.

Rhyme scheme: ABCBB. Final line 3 syllables — slows pace and gives ghostly feel.

Repetition of "and" emphasises changes and makes speaker sound angry.

Changes in physical setting and people.

The change I notice in my once own quarters!
A formal-fashioned border where the daisies used to be,
The rooms new painted, and the pictures altered,
And other cups and saucers, and no cosy nook for tea
     As with me.

10

Exclamation mark shows disbelief.

Another woman?

Sight is "dim" — barrier between living and dead.

I discern the dim faces of the sleep-wrapt servants;
They are not those who tended me through feeble hours and strong,
But strangers quite, who never knew my rule here,
Who never saw me painting, never heard my softling song
     Float along.

15

Alliteration — contrasts with "mute" dead.

Mood — ghostly voice.

We sympathise with speaker's sense of loss.

Long lines and gentle, regular rhythm give sad tone.

So I don't want to linger in this re-decked dwelling,
I feel too uneasy at the contrasts I behold,
And I make again for Mellstock to return here never,
And rejoin the roomy silence, and the mute and manifold
     Souls of old.

20

Links with line 1 — speaker returning to graveyard.

Surrounded by silent ghosts.

Thomas Hardy

POEM DICTIONARY
Mellstock — Hardy's name for the place where his first wife was buried.
mail-train — a train that carried mail during the night.
discern — make out.
softling — soft and delicate.
manifold — many and varied.

Anna Lies and Anna Tate — your perfect study buddies for poetry...

Annotate your poem in any way that works for you — underline, highlight or scribble notes. You can even use hieroglyphics if you really want to (although I wouldn't recommend it — it's very slow going).

Worked Answer

So, you've read the poem and have some ideas about how you might answer the question. The next step is to turn your scribblings into an essay plan.

Spend five minutes planning your answer

1) Always <u>plan</u> your answer <u>before</u> you start — that way, you're less likely to forget something <u>important</u>.

2) Focus on <u>three or four key quotes</u> from the poem.

3) Remember to write about <u>what</u> the poet says and <u>how</u> they say it.

4) <u>Don't</u> spend <u>too long</u> on your plan. It's only <u>rough work</u>, so you don't need to write in full sentences.

---

2. Death isn't the end

1. Intro
- Subject — a ghost visits her former home.
- Sorrow of dead.

- Ghost narrator.
- Ghost is sad, not scary — reader sympathises with her.

3. The dead are powerless
- She is "uneasy" at the changes, but can't do anything about them.
- Her only choice is to "rejoin the roomy silence".
- Sad tone (reinforced by gentle, regular rhythm) — living move on, dead don't.

(Death and the afterlife)

6. Conclusion
- Dead always with us.
- Living and dead are separate but impact on each other.

5. Effect of death on the living
- Poet vs. narrator. He imagines her response.
- Guilt at the changes/new wife?

4. Separation between dead and living
- She doesn't need the door opened — she's formless.
- Living are unaware of her.
- Living are "dim faces" — indistinct.
- Living are vocal — "softling song". Dead are "mute".

---

5) Now you've got a <u>plan</u> for your essay, you just need to <u>write</u> the thing, but today's your lucky day, because I've done this one for you...

This is how you could answer the question

Use your essay plan to make sure you answer the question.

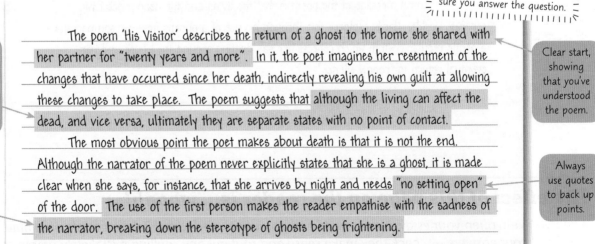

Write about the poem's main messages early on in your essay.

The poem 'His Visitor' describes the return of a ghost to the home she shared with her partner for "twenty years and more". In it, the poet imagines her resentment of the changes that have occurred since her death, indirectly revealing his own guilt at allowing these changes to take place. The poem suggests that although the living can affect the dead, and vice versa, ultimately they are separate states with no point of contact.

The most obvious point the poet makes about death is that it is not the end. Although the narrator of the poem never explicitly states that she is a ghost, it is made clear when she says, for instance, that she arrives by night and needs "no setting open" of the door. The use of the first person makes the reader empathise with the sadness of the narrator, breaking down the stereotype of ghosts being frightening.

Clear start, showing that you've understood the poem.

Always use quotes to back up points.

Give a personal response to the poem

Worked Answer

Write about feelings and mood, and use quotes to back up your points.

The feeling of sorrow is emphasised by the powerlessness of the narrator. Although she is "uneasy" at the changes that have been made to her former home, the only way she can ease her discomfort is to leave and "return here never". Death therefore involves giving up a loved home and all that is familiar, and instead accepting the loneliness that comes with joining the "roomy silence". The gentle rhythm of the poem reinforces the narrator's loneliness. The three-syllable lines that end each stanza are separated from the rest of the stanza by the change in rhythm, but they are linked to it by rhyme. They have the effect of making each stanza seem to tail off wistfully, reinforcing the narrator's sorrow, while their content shows her fixation on "before". This suggests that, while the living are able to move forward, the dead are trapped in the past.

Comment on form and the effect it has.

The poet also suggests that death divides the narrator from the living world. The colours of the poem are muted: the "grey" of night and the moon that "wastes weaker" create a feeling of unreality that contrasts with the "cosy nook" of the past. The "dim faces" of the sleeping servants may be shadowy because it is night, or because the narrator exists in the spiritual world, so to her, the material world is vague and unclear. Although the narrator is aware of her surroundings, she cannot interact with them, instead passing through the "long familiar door". The silence of the dead is emphasised by the alliteration of "mute and manifold", which contrasts with the "softling song" of the narrator when she was alive.

Think about different interpretations to help you get top marks.

Write about any imagery in the poem.

Mention and explain any poetic devices that you spot.

The poem also gives clues about the impact of death on the living. By imagining how "uneasy" the narrator feels at the "contrasts" she sees, Hardy gives the reader a hint of the guilt he feels at moving on while she cannot. The changes described are not large, but the use of an exclamation mark and the repetition of "and" in the second stanza shows how significant the poet believes they would have been to the narrator. The mention of "other cups and saucers", traditionally chosen by women, hint that the dead woman's place may have been taken by another woman. This may explain the poet's guilt. However, the fact that he is so concerned with what the ghost would feel suggests, ironically, that he has not really moved on.

Think about any hidden meanings the poem might contain.

Give a good personal response wherever you can.

Mention specific language features and explain why the poet used them.

The central message of the poem is that the living and the dead inhabit two separate worlds. Hardy explores this through his use of a ghostly first-person narrator, a gentle regular rhythm which reflects her sad drifting around the house and her eventual return to "roomy silence".

Sum up the what and how in your final paragraph.

The effect of this page on the reader is... whoah!

When you've written your essay, it's not quite time to sit back and relax. Take a couple of minutes to proofread your answers — check they make sense and root out any spelling mistakes or grammatical errors.

Comparing Two Poems

Whew, that's analysing the poem over and done with. Now it's time to tackle comparing that poem with something else. I'd have a nice cup of tea and a biscuit first if I were you.

You might have to compare two unseen poems

For more on how to structure an answer where you're comparing two poems, flick back to page 60.

1) In the exam, you'll probably have to compare <u>two unseen poems</u>, or you might have to compare <u>one unseen poem</u> with a poem from your <u>poetry anthology</u>.

2) This means that you need to write about the <u>similarities</u> and <u>differences</u> between them.

3) You'll need to discuss the <u>techniques</u> the poets use and their <u>effect on the reader</u>, so focus on the <u>structure</u>, <u>form</u> and <u>language</u> used in the two poems.

Four steps to answering a comparison question

Don't start writing <u>without thinking</u> about what you're going to say — follow these <u>four steps</u> to organise your ideas:

1) <u>Read</u> the question carefully and underline the <u>key words</u>.

2) <u>Annotate</u> the poems, focusing on the <u>techniques</u> used and how they <u>affect the reader</u>. Think about <u>similarities and differences</u> between these techniques and those used in the first poem.

3) <u>Plan</u> your answer. Identify <u>three or four</u> key <u>similarities and/or differences</u> that you're going to write about.

4) <u>Write</u> your answer. Use your plan to make sure that <u>every paragraph</u> discusses <u>one similarity or difference</u> between the <u>techniques</u> used in the two poems.

<u>R</u>ead, <u>A</u>nnotate, <u>P</u>lan, <u>W</u>rite... <u>R</u>eally <u>A</u>ngry <u>P</u>enguins <u>W</u>obble. There you go — no excuses for forgetting the four steps in the exam.

Edward was left physically unstable after a negative comment on his physique.

Here's a sample comparison question

1) <u>Before</u> you start annotating either of the poems, <u>read</u> the question carefully and highlight any <u>key words</u>.

2) Make sure that you <u>understand</u> exactly what you're being asked to do before you start writing.

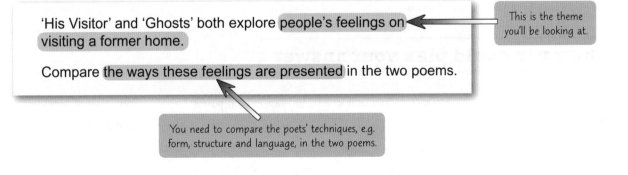

'His Visitor' and 'Ghosts' both explore people's feelings on visiting a former home.

This is the theme you'll be looking at.

Compare the ways these feelings are presented in the two poems.

You need to compare the poets' techniques, e.g. form, structure and language, in the two poems.

Two unseen poems, four useful steps — five go-oooold rings...

Comparisons can seem daunting, but if you follow the steps on this page then you'll be on the right track. Just remember to refer to both poems throughout your essay, and don't be afraid to give your own opinion.

Worked Answer

If you have to compare two poems, you'll need to read and annotate the second one, too.

Think about the first poem as you annotate the second

Read through the poem, and mark the most important bits. Remember, in your essay you need to write about the form, structure and language used in the poem and the effect they have on the reader.

Voice — first person. Similar to 'His Visitor'.

Feelings — not alone. Contrasts with loneliness in 'His Visitor'.

Contrast — emphasises present sorrow. Similar to 'His Visitor'.

Regular metre — driving, upbeat rhythm. Contrasts with 'His Visitor'.

Feelings — sadness and loss. Similar to 'His Visitor'.

Alliteration — shows bond with wife. Contrasts with loneliness in 'His Visitor'.

Subject — ghosts returning to their former home.

Feelings — yearning for the past. Similar to 'His Visitor'.

Alliteration — emphasises past happiness and warmth.

Feelings — exclamation mark shows disbelief, as in 'His Visitor'.

Regular ABAB rhyme scheme contributes to the a fast, upbeat pace.

Alliteration emphasises contrast between past and present.

Ellipsis — suggests speaker is thinking wistfully of the past.

Ghosts

I to a crumpled cabin came
Upon a hillside high,
And with me was a withered dame
As weariful as I.
5 "It used to be our home," said she;
"How I remember well!
Oh that our happy hearth should be
Today an empty shell!"

The door was flailing in the storm
10 That deafed us with its din;
The roof that kept us once so warm
Now let the snow-drift in.
The floor sagged to the sod below,
The walls caved crazily;
15 We only heard the wind of woe
Where once was glow and glee.

So there we stood disconsolate
Beneath the Midnight Dome,
And ancient miner and his mate,
20 Before our wedded home,
Where we had known such love and cheer...
I sighed, then soft she said:
"Do not regret — remember, dear,
We, too, are dead."

Robert Service

POEM DICTIONARY
deafed — deafened
sod — grass-covered earth
Midnight Dome — a mountain in Yukon Territory, Canada

This is how you could plan your answer

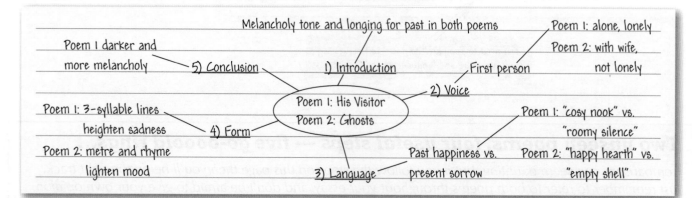

Melancholy tone and longing for past in both poems

Poem 1: alone, lonely
Poem 2: with wife, not lonely

Poem 1 darker and more melancholy

5) Conclusion   1) Introduction   First person

2) Voice

Poem 1: His Visitor
Poem 2: Ghosts

Poem 1: 3-syllable lines heighten sadness

4) Form

Poem 2: metre and rhyme lighten mood

Poem 1: "cosy nook" vs. "roomy silence"

Poem 2: "happy hearth" vs. "empty shell"

Past happiness vs. present sorrow

3) Language

Worked Answer

So, you've read the question, you've annotated both poems and you've made a cunning plan.
All you need to do now is write your essay...

This is how you could answer a comparison question

Show that you've understood the question.

'His Visitor' and 'Ghosts' are both melancholy poems in which a ghostly narrator returns to their former home and is distressed to find that it has changed dramatically. Although the poems convey similar feelings about visiting a former home, the poets use narrative voice, language and form in different ways to put these feelings across.

Explain how the techniques in the poems affect the reader.

Both poems use a first-person narrator, and in both cases this makes the narrator's feelings about their former home seem real and immediate, encouraging the reader to empathise with them. The narrator of 'His Visitor' returns home alone, and her isolation is conveyed by her repeated use of the first-person singular pronoun "I". This isolation emphasises the narrator's loneliness as she revisits the once-familiar house, now filled with "strangers". In 'Ghosts', however, the narrator is accompanied by his wife. Their close connection is highlighted by the use of the collective pronouns "we" and "us", and by the alliterative description of them as a "miner and his mate". In contrast to 'His Visitor', loneliness is not a prominent emotion in 'Ghosts', and instead Service focuses on the narrator's sadness at the destruction of his former home.

Embed short quotes into your writing.

Introduce your paragraphs with a comparison.

Both poets use language to emphasise the contrast between past happiness and present sorrow. In 'His Visitor', the "cosy nook" symbolises the warmth and comfort that the house once offered the narrator, and contrasts with the "roomy silence" of the afterlife. Similarly, in 'Ghosts' the "happy hearth" represents the joy and warmth of the past, and contrasts starkly with the "empty shell" that the house has become. In both poems, such contrasts highlight the narrators' yearning for the past. This sense of longing is further emphasised by repeated use of phrases associated with the past, such as "As before" and "used to be", suggesting that both narrators are fixated on the way things were.

Show that you understand the imagery in the poems.

Use quotes to support your argument.

The form of 'His Visitor' plays an important role in conveying the narrator's feelings. The three-syllable lines that end each stanza slow the poem's pace and give it an irregular rhythm, with each stanza trailing off wistfully. This creates a powerful sense of sadness and melancholy, which reinforces the feelings of loss and longing that are conveyed through the poem's language. In contrast, the regular metre and simple ABAB rhyme scheme of 'Ghosts' give the poem a faster pace and a driving, upbeat rhythm. The rhythm lightens the mood, making the poem seem less bleak and melancholy than 'His Visitor'.

Write about how form conveys meaning.

Summarise the similarities and differences in your conclusion.

'His Visitor' and 'Ghosts' both use language to convey similar feelings of sadness, loss and longing for the past, and regret at the changes to their former homes. However, differences in the poets' use of narrative voice and form mean that, overall, the tone of 'His Visitor' is darker and more melancholy than that of 'Ghosts'.

Remember to compare the two poems.

The reader studies with an irregular rhythm, pausing repeatedly...

Don't forget to write about both poems in every paragraph — that way you can comment on their simmerences and differalities. Just make sure you don't get them mixed up. That would be embarrassing...

Writing Well

Now on to some good old-fashioned spelling, punctuation and grammar — the examiners still love it. Writing well will improve your grade in both Language and Literature so it's important that you get it right.

Writing well will get you a better grade

A big chunk of the marks available in your English exams is for how you write, not what you write. This is what you'll be marked on:

1) Standard English
   Examiners will expect you to use standard (or formal) English (unless you're writing in the voice of a character). Don't slip into slang or local dialect — that'll make your writing harder to understand.

2) Punctuation (see pages 75-77)
   Punctuation is brilliant for making your writing smooth, clear and punchy — but only if you get it right. Make sure you know how to use commas, semicolons, apostrophes, etc. to impress the examiner.

3) Spelling (see p.79)
   Accurate spelling will get you extra marks. Learn to avoid common spelling mistakes and make sure you can spell technical words correctly, e.g. onomatopoeia, rhetorical.

4) Tenses (see p.80)
   Tenses tell your readers when things happened (i.e. in the past, present or future). Make sure you're using the right tense and be consistent — don't change tense without a good reason.

5) Sentences (see p.81)
   Sentences come in all shapes and sizes — from short and simple to long and complex. Use a mixture of correct sentence types to get the effect you want.

6) Vocabulary (see p.82)
   You'll need to use some flashy words in the exam, including technical terms and connectives. Avoid clichés (corny phrases used all the time), e.g. 'at the end of the day', and informal words like 'O.K.'

7) Paragraphs (see p.83)
   Using paragraphs lets you organise your writing into manageable sections. They can also be used to create different effects, e.g. a one-sentence paragraph can make an important point stand out.

Avoid these common mistakes

Follow these rules in the exam — otherwise it could really affect your grade.

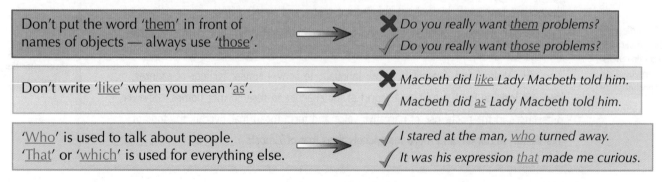

Don't put the word 'them' in front of names of objects — always use 'those'.	→	✗ Do you really want them problems? ✓ Do you really want those problems?
Don't write 'like' when you mean 'as'.	→	✗ Macbeth did like Lady Macbeth told him. ✓ Macbeth did as Lady Macbeth told him.
'Who' is used to talk about people. 'That' or 'which' is used for everything else.	→	✓ I stared at the man, who turned away. ✓ It was his expression that made me curious.

Writing and speaking bad English won't get you nowhere...

It's true. I can't stand people what can't speak and write English proper... (cough). But seriously — this is important stuff. It's not the most exciting topic in the world, but then I can't let you have too much fun...

Punctuation

Punctuation isn't just there to make your essays look pretty — it also makes them easier to understand. The more accurate your punctuation is in the exam, the clearer your answers will be.

Start and finish your sentences correctly

Always <u>start</u> sentences with a <u>capital letter</u>. Sentences always <u>end</u> with either:

- a <u>full stop</u> — use these for most sentences, especially in formal writing.

- a <u>question mark</u> — use these if the sentence is asking a question.

- an <u>exclamation mark</u> — use these if you want your sentence to have a strong impact.

*Juan ends every
sentence with a paws.*

All these ways of ending a sentence mark a definite <u>pause</u> before the next sentence starts.

Use commas to put pauses in sentences

Commas are a great way to improve the way your writing flows.

1) Commas are used to <u>separate</u> the parts of long sentences so that the meaning is clear. For example:

In the valley below, the villages seemed very small. ⟹ Without the comma, the sentence would begin 'In the valley below the villages'.

2) Commas are also used to <u>break up</u> items in a <u>list</u>:

The waves reared, twisted, leapt and raged around the stricken boat. ⟹ The commas separate the different <u>verbs</u> listed in the sentence.

In a list, the last two items are always separated by a connective instead of a comma.

3) <u>Pairs of commas</u> work like brackets to add <u>extra information</u> to the <u>middle</u> of sentences:

The novel, despite its melancholy start, finishes on an optimistic note. ⟹ The sentence would <u>still work</u> without the bit in the middle.

Colons and semicolons link parts of a sentence

1) Colons are used to <u>link</u> parts of a sentence if the second part <u>explains</u> the first part:

The mood of the poem changes towards the end: it becomes much more solemn. ⟹ You should only use a colon if the first part <u>leads on to</u> the second part.

2) Semicolons are used to turn <u>two related sentences</u> into one. Both sentences must be about the <u>same thing</u> and must make sense <u>on their own</u>. A semicolon marks a stronger pause than a comma:

Immigration was a source of tension in the 1950s; the novel's language reflects this. ⟹ The parts on either side of the semicolon are <u>connected</u> and <u>equally important.</u>

CGP — putting the 'pun' in 'punctuation' since 1995...

lordy lordy just think how hard it would be to read something without punctuation it would drive you up the wall wouldn't it and it's exactly the same for the examiners they can't stand it at all so use it I tell you

Apostrophes

Loads of people get apostrophes wrong, but they're actually not that hard. You just need to learn a few rules.

Add an apostrophe to show who owns something

1) Apostrophes show when something <u>belongs</u> to someone or something.

> The <u>writer's</u> tone is aggressive. ⟹ The tone <u>belonging</u> to the writer is aggressive.

2) There's one exception to this rule: '<u>it's</u>' <u>with</u> an apostrophe is short for 'it is' or 'it has' — '<u>its</u>' <u>never</u> has an apostrophe to show belonging.

> The elephant lifted <u>its gnarled trunk</u> and lumbered slowly away. ⟹ The trunk belongs to the elephant, so 'its' <u>doesn't</u> have an apostrophe.

If you're writing a plural word, just add 's', 'es' or whatever to the end — never use an apostrophe to show something's plural.

It gets a bit tricky with groups of people or things

There are two golden rules here:

1) If a plural already ends in <u>s</u>, you need to stick an apostrophe on the <u>end</u> to show possession.

> The <u>boys'</u> heart rates quickened as they heard the car approaching. ⟹ There is more than one boy, so the apostrophe needs to go <u>after</u> the 's'.

2) If the plural doesn't end in <u>s</u> (for example mice, men, women, sheep), just follow the <u>normal rule</u>.

> The <u>men's</u> authority is undermined in the play. ⟹ The word 'men' is already plural, so just add an apostrophe and 's' <u>to the end</u>.

Apostrophes can show where there's a missing letter

You can <u>shorten</u> some pairs of words by sticking them together and cutting out letters — as long as you <u>replace</u> those letters with an apostrophe.

> I am → I'm ⟹ The letter 'a' has been removed, so an apostrophe goes <u>in its place</u>.

Here are some common examples of words that need an <u>apostrophe</u>:

They are	→ They're	Does not	→ Doesn't	Will not	→ <u>Won't</u>
They have	→ They've	Cannot	→ Can't	I would	→ I'd
Who is	→ Who's	We are	→ We're	I had	→ I'd
Do not	→ Don't	We will	→ We'll	It is	→ It's

<u>Won't</u> doesn't quite follow the rule. 'Willn't' would sound a bit silly, I suppose.

Apostrophe — the well-known Greek philosopher...

You need apostrophes in your life. Just think how some classic songs would sound without them —
"Do not stop me now, I am having such a good time, I am having a ball..." (Ahh, I know you are. Me too.).

Speech Marks

I know you're probably fed up of me talking, so now you can read about <u>other people</u> talking.

Speech marks show that someone's speaking

1) Speech marks (or <u>quotation</u> marks) mark the <u>start</u> and <u>end</u> of what someone has said.

> *"You're going to regret that," growled Tom.* ⟹ Tom's speech begins on 'You're' and ends on 'that'.

2) You need to start a new <u>paragraph</u> every time a new person speaks.

> *"What makes you think I'll regret it?" asked Arthur.*
> *"I could make your life very difficult," replied Tom.* ⟶ When Tom replies to Arthur, the writer starts a new paragraph.

To see how to use quotation marks to quote from texts, flick to page 44.

Always start speech with a capital letter

1) <u>Speech</u> always starts with a capital letter — even if it doesn't begin the sentence.

> *Arthur muttered, "<u>You</u> think you're untouchable. I'm not afraid of you."* ⟶ 'You' starts with a capital letter, even though it's in the middle of the sentence.

2) If speech is split into two sections, you <u>don't</u> need a capital letter at the start of the second section.

> *"You should be afraid of me," Tom sneered, "<u>because</u> everybody else is."* ⟶ Tom's speech is interrupted by the narration, so 'because' doesn't need a capital letter.

End speech with a punctuation mark

When you put punctuation at the end of your speech, it should go <u>before</u> the speech mark.

1) Spoken questions end with a <u>question mark</u>, and exclamations with an <u>exclamation mark</u>.

> *"Why do you think that <u>is?</u>" asked Arthur.*
> *"You know full <u>well!</u>" shouted Tom.* ⟶ The punctuation goes at the end of the speech, but before the speech marks.

2) If the speech has finished but the sentence hasn't, use a <u>comma</u>.

> *"You'll never be able to prove that I'm responsible for Jo's <u>disappearance</u>," Tom jeered.* ⟶ Tom's speech has finished but the sentence hasn't, so 'disappearance' is followed by a comma.

3) If the speech ends the sentence and it <u>isn't</u> a question or an exclamation, you need a <u>full stop</u>.

> *Arthur replied softly, "I've been recording this conversation, and you just gave me all the proof I <u>need</u>."* ⟶ Here, the full stop ends the sentence.

You'll thank me one day — mark my words...

Actually remembering to use speech marks is easy enough — it's working out where all the punctuation goes that's the problem. Practise before the exam so that you get into good habits before it really counts.

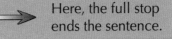

Negatives

I'll pass on some advice my granpappy gave to me — he sat me down on his knee one day and said, "Now don't you go using no double negatives, you hear." My granpappy was a wise man.

'No' isn't the only negative word

1) The easiest way to make a phrase negative is to add '<u>no</u>' or '<u>not</u>'.

> There *is* a logical solution to the situation.   ⟹   There *is no* logical solution to the situation.
>
> The poem *is* written in free verse.   ⟹   The poem *is not* written in free verse.

2) Words ending in <u>-n't</u> are also negative.

> This argument *has* got a lot of credibility.   ⟹   This argument *hasn't* got a lot of credibility.

Don't use a double negative

Words ending in '<u>-n't</u>' are <u>negative</u>, so you <u>don't</u> need to add '<u>no</u>' or '<u>not</u>'.

> *I <u>don't</u> agree with <u>no</u> politicians.*   ⟶   This really means 'I <u>do</u> agree with politicians'. <u>Two negative words</u> in the same phrase make it <u>positive</u>. You should only use <u>one negative</u> at a time.

People call me overly negative — they don't know nothing.

© iStockphoto.com/uzuri71

The word 'none' has different meanings

1) '<u>None</u>' is a word that can cause problems. As a <u>pronoun</u> it means '<u>not one</u>' or '<u>not any</u>':

> *<u>None</u> of my friends came to see me off.*   ⟹   Here, 'None' means '<u>not one</u>'.

> *There are <u>none</u> of these techniques in the poem.*   ⟹   Here, 'none' means '<u>not any</u>'.

2) 'None' can also mean '<u>not at all</u>':

> *The house was <u>none</u> the worse for its faded paint and weather-beaten feel; it only added to the building's charm.*   ⟶   This means that the appearance of the house doesn't make it worse <u>at all</u>.

3) 'None' should <u>not</u> be used with other negative words:

> ✘ *He's <u>not</u> got <u>none</u>.*   ⟹   Remember the <u>double negative</u> rule — this really means 'He's got some'.
>
> ✓ *He has <u>none</u>.*   ⟹   This is correct — it means 'He hasn't got any'.

Stop being so negative — it's not that bad...

Two negatives make a positive — hang on a sec, I thought this was an English book, not a Maths book. Next thing you know you'll have to study Pythagoras' first novel as part of GCSE English.

Spelling

I knew an English examiner once. He told me that the thing he hated most in the world was...
(dramatic pause)... gravy. But he said he didn't like bad spelling either.

Don't confuse different words that sound the same

Words that <u>sound</u> similar can mean completely different things. Here are some common examples:

effect/affect

1) <u>Effect</u> is a <u>noun</u> — it is the result of an action.   ⟹ *The emotive language has a powerful <u>effect</u> on the reader.*

2) <u>Affect</u> is a <u>verb</u> meaning to act on or influence something.   ⟹ *Dim lighting <u>affects</u> the mood of the scene.*

practise/practice

1) <u>Practise</u> is a <u>verb</u>. ⟹ *He <u>practised</u> his lines until his head swam.*

2) <u>Practice</u> is a <u>noun</u>. ⟹ *The <u>practice</u> of fox hunting is cruel and unnecessary.*

where/were/wear

1) <u>Where</u> is used to talk about <u>place</u> and position. ⟹ *<u>Where</u> had she seen that symbol before?*

2) <u>Were</u> is a past tense form of the verb '<u>to be</u>'. ⟹ *The boys <u>were</u> hiding behind a statue.*

3) <u>Wear</u> is a <u>verb</u> used with clothes, hair, jewellery etc. ⟹ *He <u>wears</u> armour of burnished gold.*

there/their/they're

1) <u>There</u> is used for <u>place</u> and position. ⟹ *Jo dived behind the sofa and waited <u>there</u>, listening hard.*

2) <u>Their</u> shows <u>possession</u>. ⟹ *Both poets use metaphors to emphasise <u>their</u> message.*

3) <u>They're</u> is the short form of '<u>they are</u>'. ⟹ *<u>They're</u> the most dramatic lines in the play.*

Watch out for these common spelling mistakes

1) Words can have <u>silent</u> letters. Some silent letters are commonly found at the <u>start</u> of words (e.g. '<u>k</u>n' and '<u>w</u>r') and others are often found at the <u>end</u> of words (e.g. '<u>bt</u>' and 'm<u>n</u>').

> *know, knock, write, wrong, doubt, debt, solemn, autumn.* ⟹ You don't say these letters, but you must write them.

2) Some words <u>change</u> their spelling when you add a <u>suffix</u>. A suffix is a letter or group of letters put onto the end of a word to change its meaning, e.g. '-y', '-ment', '-ing'.

Humour ⟹ Humorous	Big ⟹ Biggest	Hurry ⟹ Hurried
Die ⟹ Dying	Mimic ⟹ Mimicking	Argue ⟹ Argument

3) Make sure you know which words use '<u>ie</u>' (e.g. p<u>ie</u>ce, bel<u>ie</u>ve) and which use '<u>ei</u>' (e.g. th<u>ei</u>r, rec<u>ei</u>ve).

Get your spelling write...

Watch out for tricky writers' names and technical terms too — your essays will be much less convincing (and you'll miss out on some easy marks) if you've misspelled 'Shakespeare' or 'onomatopoeia'.

Types of Words

"The poem is full of descriptive adverbs," sounds about five grades better than, "There are lots of nice words" Make sure you know your pronouns from your adjectives and refer to them by name in the exam.

Every word in a sentence has its own job

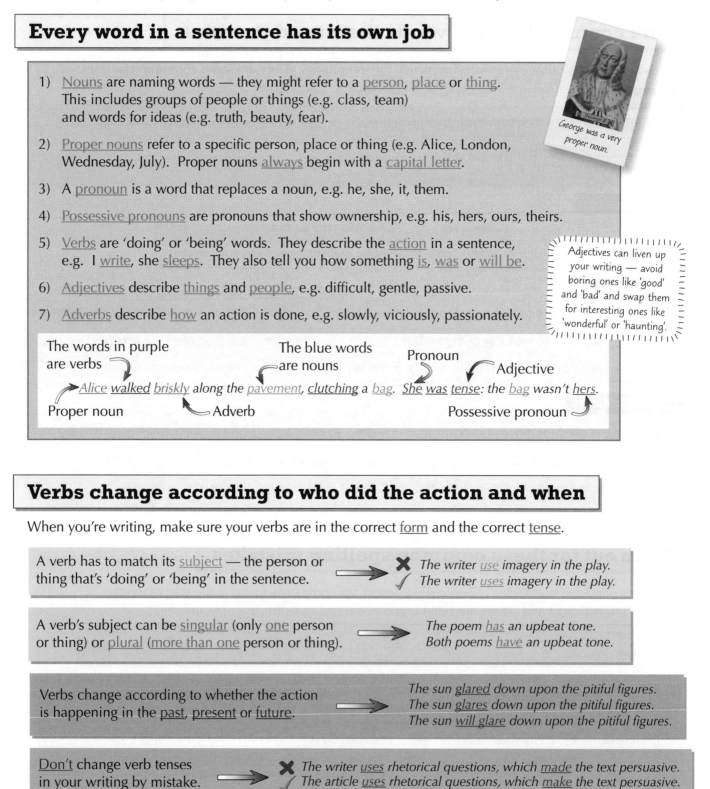

1) <u>Nouns</u> are naming words — they might refer to a <u>person</u>, <u>place</u> or <u>thing</u>. This includes groups of people or things (e.g. class, team) and words for ideas (e.g. truth, beauty, fear).

2) <u>Proper nouns</u> refer to a specific person, place or thing (e.g. Alice, London, Wednesday, July). Proper nouns <u>always</u> begin with a <u>capital letter</u>.

3) A <u>pronoun</u> is a word that replaces a noun, e.g. he, she, it, them.

4) <u>Possessive pronouns</u> are pronouns that show ownership, e.g. his, hers, ours, theirs.

5) <u>Verbs</u> are 'doing' or 'being' words. They describe the <u>action</u> in a sentence, e.g. I <u>write</u>, she <u>sleeps</u>. They also tell you how something <u>is</u>, <u>was</u> or <u>will be</u>.

6) <u>Adjectives</u> describe <u>things</u> and <u>people</u>, e.g. difficult, gentle, passive.

7) <u>Adverbs</u> describe <u>how</u> an action is done, e.g. slowly, viciously, passionately.

George was a very proper noun.

Adjectives can liven up your writing — avoid boring ones like 'good' and 'bad' and swap them for interesting ones like 'wonderful' or 'haunting'.

The words in purple are verbs

The blue words are nouns

Pronoun

Adjective

Alice walked briskly along the pavement, clutching a bag. She was tense: the bag wasn't hers.

Proper noun

Adverb

Possessive pronoun

Verbs change according to who did the action and when

When you're writing, make sure your verbs are in the correct <u>form</u> and the correct <u>tense</u>.

A verb has to match its <u>subject</u> — the person or thing that's 'doing' or 'being' in the sentence.

✗ *The writer <u>use</u> imagery in the play.*
✓ *The writer <u>uses</u> imagery in the play.*

A verb's subject can be <u>singular</u> (only <u>one</u> person or thing) or <u>plural</u> (<u>more than one</u> person or thing).

The poem <u>has</u> an upbeat tone.
Both poems <u>have</u> an upbeat tone.

Verbs change according to whether the action is happening in the <u>past</u>, <u>present</u> or <u>future</u>.

The sun <u>glared</u> down upon the pitiful figures.
The sun <u>glares</u> down upon the pitiful figures.
The sun <u>will glare</u> down upon the pitiful figures.

<u>Don't</u> change verb tenses in your writing by mistake.

✗ *The writer <u>uses</u> rhetorical questions, which <u>made</u> the text persuasive.*
✓ *The article <u>uses</u> rhetorical questions, which <u>make</u> the text persuasive.*

This is so boring — I'm going to make adverbal complaint...

If you're unsure about which word to choose, say your sentence out loud and decide whether it sounds right. I'd avoid doing this in the actual exam though — random shouting out tends to be frowned upon...

Sentences

If you're looking for top marks, you need to think about varying your sentences and ordering them logically.

Vary the style of your sentences

The examiners will be impressed if you use a mixture of sentence types <u>effectively</u>. There are <u>three main types</u> to choose from:

Including the odd question or command in your writing can help the reader feel more involved.

1) A <u>simple sentence</u> has a subject and <u>one</u> main verb.

> *The text focuses on life in India.* 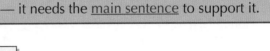 The <u>subject</u> here is 'the text' and the <u>verb</u> is 'focuses'.

2) A <u>compound sentence</u> usually has <u>two or more</u> parts, each containing a verb. The parts are linked together by words such as <u>and</u> or <u>but</u>.

> *He <u>smashed</u> the window and <u>tumbled</u> out of the building.* ⟹ The subject 'he' is <u>shared</u> by both verbs.

> *<u>Byron</u> uses metaphors, but <u>Hardy</u> uses similes.* ⟹ These two verbs have <u>different</u> subjects — 'Byron' in the first part, 'Hardy' in the second.

3) A <u>complex sentence</u> contains a part that wouldn't make sense on its own. This part is joined to the main sentence by a word like <u>if</u>, <u>as</u>, <u>because</u> or <u>although</u>.

> *<u>Because the protagonist dies</u>, the reader feels a sense of despair at the end of the novel.* ⟹ The underlined part <u>wouldn't work</u> on its own — it needs the <u>main sentence</u> to support it.

Start your sentences in different ways

<u>Varying</u> the <u>beginning</u> of your sentences makes your writing more <u>interesting</u> to read.

> *<u>There</u> was a chill in the air as Jo walked towards the house. <u>There</u> was nobody around. <u>There</u> was a big oak door and Jo knocked on it.* ⟹ This extract is <u>boring</u> because all the sentences begin in the same way.

> *<u>There</u> was a chill in the air as Jo walked towards the house. <u>Nobody</u> was around. <u>Jo</u> knocked on the big oak door.* ⟹ This extract is more <u>interesting</u> because the sentences start in different ways.

Chronological order makes things easy to follow

Your sentences need to be in a sensible <u>order</u> — if the examiner can't follow them easily you'll miss out on marks. <u>Chronological order</u> (the order in which things happened) is the most logical order to write in.

> *James flung himself sideways and rolled into a bush. He was running away because the man had started chasing him. As he had run around the corner he had seen the bush — it was the perfect hiding place.* 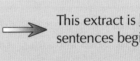 The sentences <u>aren't</u> in chronological order, so it's <u>not clear</u> what's happening.

> *James flew around the corner, running hard. The man pursuing him was catching up — he'd never make it. Suddenly, he flung himself sideways and rolled, unnoticed, into a bush.* ⟹ The sentences <u>are</u> in chronological order so this is <u>easy</u> to follow.

Variety is the spice of life — send of exam papers too...

This page is your one-way ticket to sophisticated writing. Varying your sentence types will make your answers a whole lot more interesting — not just for you, but for the examiner too.

Writing Varied Sentences

I'll tell you where to find a couple more tricks that'll help win the examiner over.
But I can only whisper it. So come a bit closer... a bit closer... that's it... they're here on this page — where else would they be?

Use descriptive language to make your writing interesting

Descriptive language creates interesting <u>visual images</u> for the reader.

1) You could compare two things using less than, more than, etc.

> The lace was <u>more delicate</u> <u>than</u> a finely spun web.
>
> It was <u>colder than</u> an Arctic winter.
>
> She was the <u>most beautiful</u> woman in Millom.

→ These descriptions are <u>more</u> interesting than saying 'it was more delicate', 'it was very cold' or 'she was beautiful'.

When you compare, either say "more than..." or "the most...", or use the form of the word that ends in "er" or "est". Don't do both.

2) You could use a <u>simile</u> (saying one thing is <u>like</u> another).

> Beth felt <u>as</u> happy <u>as</u> a hippo in a mud pool.
>
> I'd forgotten my gloves and my fingers were <u>like</u> blocks of ice.

→ Similes usually use the words 'like' or 'as' to compare one thing to another.

3) You could use a <u>metaphor</u> (describing one thing as if it <u>is</u> something else). There needs to be an <u>obvious link</u> between the thing you're talking about and the metaphor you're using to describe it.

> John's face <u>was</u> a waxen mask that betrayed no emotion.

→ John's face wasn't literally a mask, but the language creates a <u>strong visual image</u>.

Use different words for the same thing

1) Don't fall into the trap of using the same <u>adjectives</u> all the time — especially vague ones like "<u>nice</u>" or "<u>weird</u>".

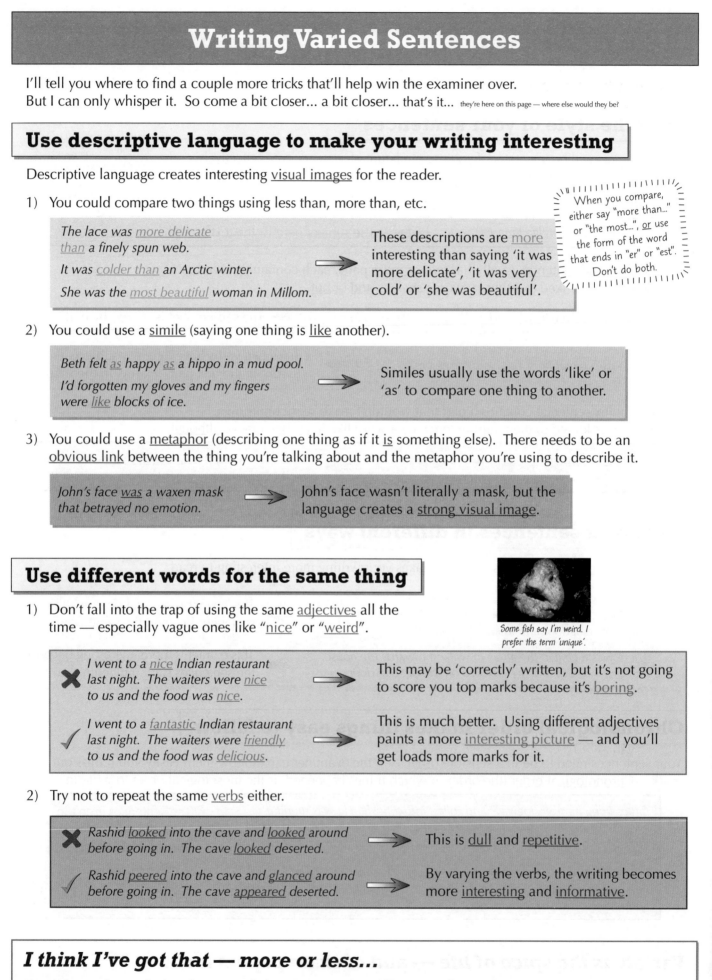

Some fish say I'm weird. I prefer the term 'unique'.

> ✗ I went to a <u>nice</u> Indian restaurant last night. The waiters were <u>nice</u> to us and the food was <u>nice</u>.

→ This may be 'correctly' written, but it's not going to score you top marks because it's <u>boring</u>.

> ✓ I went to a <u>fantastic</u> Indian restaurant last night. The waiters were <u>friendly</u> to us and the food was <u>delicious</u>.

→ This is much better. Using different adjectives paints a more <u>interesting picture</u> — and you'll get loads more marks for it.

2) Try not to repeat the same <u>verbs</u> either.

> ✗ Rashid <u>looked</u> into the cave and <u>looked</u> around before going in. The cave <u>looked</u> deserted.

→ This is <u>dull</u> and <u>repetitive</u>.

> ✓ Rashid <u>peered</u> into the cave and <u>glanced</u> around before going in. The cave <u>appeared</u> deserted.

→ By varying the verbs, the writing becomes more <u>interesting</u> and <u>informative</u>.

I think I've got that — more or less...

Don't forget that including fancy words from time to time will impress the examiner, especially if you can use and spell them correctly. You'll earn yourself some more marks, too — how stupendously phenomenal.

Paragraphs

In the heat of the exam it's easy to forget to start new paragraphs, but they're key to getting a good grade.

Start a new paragraph every time something changes

All the sentences in a paragraph should be <u>related</u> to each other. That means you need to start a new paragraph every time <u>something new</u> is introduced. For example:

1) When you introduce a new <u>person</u>.

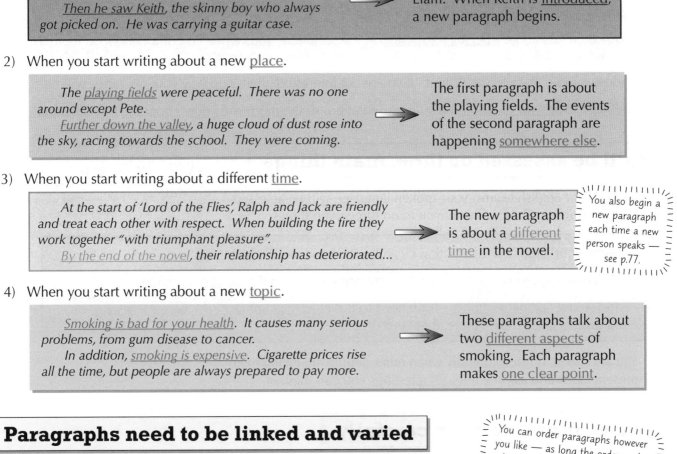

> <u>*Horrified, Liam*</u> *sank to the floor. His guitar was broken and he was due on stage in two minutes.*
> <u>*Then he saw Keith*</u>*, the skinny boy who always got picked on. He was carrying a guitar case.*

⟶ The first paragraph is about Liam. When Keith is <u>introduced</u>, a new paragraph begins.

2) When you start writing about a new <u>place</u>.

> *The <u>playing fields</u> were peaceful. There was no one around except Pete.*
> <u>*Further down the valley*</u>*, a huge cloud of dust rose into the sky, racing towards the school. They were coming.*

⟶ The first paragraph is about the playing fields. The events of the second paragraph are happening <u>somewhere else</u>.

3) When you start writing about a different <u>time</u>.

> *At the start of 'Lord of the Flies', Ralph and Jack are friendly and treat each other with respect. When building the fire they work together "with triumphant pleasure".*
> <u>*By the end of the novel*</u>*, their relationship has deteriorated...*

⟶ The new paragraph is about a <u>different time</u> in the novel.

You also begin a new paragraph each time a new person speaks — see p.77.

4) When you start writing about a new <u>topic</u>.

> <u>*Smoking is bad for your health*</u>*. It causes many serious problems, from gum disease to cancer.*
> *In addition, <u>smoking is expensive</u>. Cigarette prices rise all the time, but people are always prepared to pay more.*

⟶ These paragraphs talk about two <u>different aspects</u> of smoking. Each paragraph makes <u>one clear point</u>.

Paragraphs need to be linked and varied

You can order paragraphs however you like — as long the order you've chosen makes sense to the reader.

1) You've got to <u>link</u> every paragraph with the one before and the one after.

- You could use <u>connectives</u> (linking words) — therefore, however, on the other hand etc.

- Or you could <u>refer back</u> to something you've said in the one above.

> *Terrorism plays a huge role in society today. We can't turn on the news without feeling threatened or <u>afraid</u>.*
> *Is a world where violence and <u>fear</u> are commonplace really one we want our children to grow up in?*

⟶ The 'fear' in the second paragraph <u>refers back</u> to feeling 'afraid' in the first paragraph.

2) Don't make your paragraphs too repetitive — try starting with a <u>rhetorical question</u> like the example above, or create a <u>one-sentence paragraph</u> for effect.

Paragraphs — out with the old, and in with the new...

Paragraphs give structure to your answer and break it into separate points so it's easier to read. You can also use them creatively to make your work that bit more interesting — the trick is to vary their structure.

Spoken Language Assessment

The Spoken Language assessment is all about communicating effectively and clearly in front of an audience. It can seem quite daunting, but you'll feel a whole lot better if you're fully prepared for it.

You'll have to give a presentation

1) You'll be given a task — this is usually delivering a <u>presentation</u> or a <u>speech</u>. Your teacher might give you some guidelines, but normally you can <u>choose</u> your own topic.

You might be able to use visual prompts, for example pictures or slides — check with your teacher.

- You could talk about a subject you're <u>interested</u> in, e.g. a type of music you like or a sport you play.
- You might discuss something that <u>concerns</u> you, e.g. addiction to social media or underage drinking.
- You could give your opinion on a <u>current topic</u>, e.g. a news story or a new rule proposed at your school.
- You could talk about a <u>personal experience</u>, e.g. a holiday you've been on or a childhood memory.

2) Choose a topic that you <u>care</u> about. If you're not interested, there's <u>no way</u> your audience will be.

3) You need to <u>answer questions</u> on your presentation, so the <u>more</u> you know about the topic, the <u>better</u>.

You'll be assessed on three main things

1) Unlike your English exams, your spoken language will be assessed by your <u>teacher</u>. They will want you to do <u>three</u> main things:

The Spoken Language assessment doesn't affect your English Language grade — you get a separate result for it.

- Present your ideas and information <u>clearly</u> — this will usually be to your <u>class</u> and your <u>teacher</u>.
- <u>Listen</u> to any questions or feedback for your presentation and <u>reply appropriately</u>.
- Speak using <u>Standard English</u> — you need to use <u>correct grammar</u> and avoid <u>slang</u>. There's more about this on p.85.

2) You also need to <u>listen carefully</u> when other people are giving their presentations and ask any <u>relevant questions</u> you can think of.

Plan your presentation carefully

There aren't any hard and fast rules about how to put together your task, but <u>planning properly</u> is essential.

1) Work out what your <u>purpose</u> is and how to <u>achieve</u> it — for example, if you're trying to <u>persuade</u> your audience to agree with your point of view, you should use some <u>rhetorical devices</u> (see pages 18 and 34).

Writing a speech is like writing a non-fiction text — Section Four gives you some tips on how to do this.

2) Think about what to include — research any <u>facts</u> or <u>statistics</u> that you can use to <u>support</u> your argument or add <u>interest</u> to your speech.

3) Decide how to <u>structure</u> your presentation:

- Make sure you have a clear <u>introduction</u> stating the <u>topic</u> you've chosen. If you're putting across an argument, let the audience know your <u>point of view</u>.
- Plan what <u>order</u> to cover your points in. For example, if you're discussing a topic, you might give all your points <u>for</u> it, followed by all your points <u>against</u>.
- End your presentation with a <u>strong conclusion</u> — this could sum up the <u>key points</u> of your speech, or give your <u>own opinion</u> on the subject.

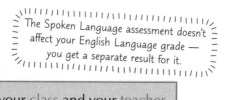

When John was told "plan it", his presentation really took off.

Spoken Language Assessment

Make sure you speak clearly

Your presentation needs to be easy for your audience to follow
— make sure you <u>speak clearly</u> and follow a <u>clear structure</u>.

Speak up and look around the room when you're talking — that way everyone can hear you.

1) Choose your vocabulary carefully so it's <u>suitable</u> for your audience.

> ✗ *International media conglomerates make the movie industry monotonous.*
>
> ➡ The vocabulary is <u>too technical</u> and makes the sentence hard to follow.
>
> ✓ *Large film companies make the movie industry bland.*
>
> ➡ These words are <u>simpler</u>, so the sentence is easier to understand.

2) Don't repeat yourself unless you're doing it for <u>effect</u>. Keep your points <u>concise</u> — stating them again in different words wastes valuable time.

> ✗ *We might succeed because we might be able to do what we need to, but we might also fail if we don't do what we need to. We'll only know once we succeed or fail.*
>
> ➡ This is <u>waffly</u> and <u>repetitive</u>, which makes it sound <u>dull</u>.
>
> ✓ *Perhaps we'll succeed. Perhaps we'll fail. Only time will tell.*
>
> ➡ Here, repetition is used for <u>effect</u> — it helps the speaker make a <u>strong, memorable point</u>.

3) Draw attention to the most important <u>facts</u>. Then the audience will remember them.

> *One and a half acres of forest is cut down every second — that's <u>the size of 66 football pitches</u>.*
>
> ➡ Linking a statistic to something the audience <u>can relate to</u> makes it more <u>memorable</u>.

Use Standard English

<u>Standard English</u> means <u>formal</u> English — the kind of language you'd use in an essay. You need to <u>speak</u> in Standard English when you do your <u>speech</u> or <u>presentation</u>.

Grammar mistakes are easy enough to avoid once you know how — see pages 74 and 78 for some common errors.

1) Don't speak in the <u>informal way</u> you might when talking to your friends.

> ✗ *Some people are, like, "P.E. is completely pointless".*
> ➡ This is too <u>informal</u> and <u>familiar</u>.
>
> ✓ *Some people maintain that P.E. is completely pointless.*
> ➡ This is much better.

2) Don't use <u>slang</u> or <u>local dialect</u> words that some people might not understand.

> ✗ *Local residents were <u>gutted</u> at the decision.*
> ➡ "Gutted" is a <u>slang</u> term.
>
> ✓ *Local residents were <u>disappointed</u> with the decision.*
> ➡ The <u>formal</u> wording is more appropriate.

3) Use <u>correct grammar</u>.

> ✗ *The issue <u>ain't</u> high on the political agenda.*
> ➡ This sentence is <u>grammatically incorrect</u>.
>
> ✓ *The issue <u>isn't</u> high on the political agenda.*
> ➡ The word 'isn't' is correct here.

Standard English — when you don't have room for a Full English...

If you're worried about sticking to the point, scribbling some notes will help you to keep on track. Don't write out every single word you want to say — you'll end up sounding like a robot. Just jot down the essentials.

Glossary

alliteration	When words that are <u>close together</u> start with the <u>same sound</u>. E.g. "the <u>b</u>eat of the <u>b</u>and".
ambiguity	Where a word or phrase has <u>two or more</u> possible <u>interpretations</u>.
analogy	A <u>comparison</u> to show how one thing is <u>similar</u> to another, which makes it easier to <u>understand</u> or more <u>memorable</u>. E.g. "the human brain is like a super-computer: complex and powerful."
antithesis	A <u>rhetorical technique</u> where <u>opposing</u> words or ideas are put <u>together</u> to show a contrast.
aside	When a <u>character</u> in a play makes a <u>short comment</u> that reveals their <u>thoughts</u> to the <u>audience</u>, and no other character can hear it.
assonance	When words share the same <u>vowel sound</u> but their consonants are different, e.g. "in this d<u>ee</u>p joy to s<u>ee</u> and hear th<u>ee</u>".
audience	The <u>person</u> or <u>group of people</u> that read or listen to a text.
autobiographical	Describing something that happened in the <u>writer's life</u>.
biased writing	Writing that gives <u>more support</u> to one point of view than to another.
blank verse	Lines from a play or poem that are written in <u>iambic pentameter</u> and <u>don't rhyme</u>.
broadsheet	A <u>formal</u> type of newspaper, which often focuses on more <u>serious</u> topics, e.g. *The Guardian*.
caesura (plural <u>caesurae</u>)	A <u>pause</u> in a line of poetry. E.g. the full stop in "Over the drifted stream. My father spins" in 'Eden Rock' by Charles Causley.
chronological	When events are arranged in the <u>order</u> in which they <u>happened</u>.
cinematic writing	Writing that makes the reader feel like they're watching a <u>film</u>.
clause	Part of a sentence that has a <u>subject</u> and a <u>verb</u>. <u>Main clauses</u> make sense on their own.
colloquial language	<u>Informal</u> language that sounds like ordinary <u>speech</u>, e.g. "with your pals".
commentary (newspaper article)	A type of newspaper article that expresses the <u>opinions</u> of the writer on a theme or news event. Also called a <u>column</u> or <u>opinion piece</u>.
complex sentence	A sentence that contains <u>one or more subordinate clauses</u>.
compound sentence	Two <u>main clauses</u> joined to make one sentence using a <u>conjunction</u> such as 'but', 'and' or 'so'. E.g. "The cat came in, <u>so</u> the dog left the room."
connotations	The <u>suggestions</u> that words can make <u>beyond</u> their obvious meaning. E.g. 'stroll' means 'walk', but it has connotations of moving slowly.
consonance	<u>Repetition</u> of a <u>consonant sound</u> in nearby words, e.g. "And fi<u>t</u> the brigh<u>t</u> s<u>t</u>eel-poin<u>t</u>ed sock".
context	The <u>background</u> to something, or the situation <u>surrounding</u> it, which affects the way it's understood. E.g. the context of a text from 1915 would include the First World War.
counter-argument	The <u>opposite</u> point of view to the writer's own view. This is useful when writing to argue or persuade — first give the counter-argument, then explain why you <u>disagree</u> with it.
direct address	When a narrator or writer <u>speaks directly</u> to another character or to the reader, e.g. "you might recall..."
double negative	A sentence construction that <u>incorrectly</u> expresses a <u>negative idea</u> by using <u>two</u> negative words or phrases, e.g. "I <u>don't</u> want <u>no</u> trouble."
dramatic monologue	A <u>form</u> of poetry that uses the assumed voice of a <u>single speaker</u> who is <u>not the poet</u> to address an <u>implied audience</u>.

Glossary

Glossary

emotive	Something that makes you <u>feel</u> a particular <u>emotion</u>.
empathy	The ability to <u>imagine</u> and <u>understand</u> someone else's <u>feelings</u> or <u>experiences</u>.
end-stopping	Finishing a line of poetry with the <u>end</u> of a <u>phrase or sentence</u>, usually marked by punctuation.
enjambment	When a sentence or phrase runs over from <u>one line</u> or <u>stanza</u> to the <u>next</u>.
explicit information	Information that's <u>directly stated</u> in a text.
figurative language	Language that is used in a <u>non-literal</u> way to create an effect, e.g. personification.
first person	A <u>narrative viewpoint</u> where the narrator is one of the <u>characters</u>, written using words like 'I', 'me', 'we' and 'our'.
flashback	A writing technique where the scene shifts from the <u>present</u> to an event in the <u>past</u>.
foreshadowing	A literary device where a writer <u>hints</u> or <u>gives clues</u> about a <u>future event</u>.
form	The <u>type</u> of text (e.g. a letter, a speech) or poem (e.g. a sonnet or a ballad).
frame narrative	A narrative in which one story is presented <u>within</u> another.
free verse	Poetry that <u>doesn't rhyme</u> and has <u>no regular rhythm</u> or <u>line length</u>.
generalisation	A statement that gives an <u>overall impression</u> (sometimes a misleading one), without going into details. E.g. "children today eat too much junk food."
half-rhymes	Words that have a <u>similar</u>, but not identical, <u>end sound</u>. E.g. "plough" and "follow".
hyperbole	When <u>exaggeration</u> is used to have an <u>effect</u> on the reader.
iambic pentameter	Poetry with a <u>metre</u> of <u>ten syllables</u> — five of them stressed, and five unstressed. The <u>stress</u> falls on <u>every second syllable</u>, e.g. "And <u>full</u>-grown <u>lambs</u> loud <u>bleat</u> from <u>hill</u>y <u>bourn</u>".
imagery	Language that creates a <u>picture in your mind</u>, e.g. <u>metaphors</u>, <u>similes</u> and <u>personification</u>.
imperative verb	A verb that gives orders or directions, e.g. "<u>run</u> away" or "<u>stop</u> that".
impersonal tone	A tone of writing that <u>doesn't</u> try to directly <u>engage</u> with the reader.
implicit information	Information that's hinted at <u>without</u> being said outright.
inference	A <u>conclusion</u> reached about something, based on <u>evidence</u>. E.g. from the sentence "Yasmin wrinkled her nose at the lasagne", you could <u>infer</u> that Yasmin doesn't like lasagne.
internal rhyme	When two or more words in the <u>same line</u> rhyme, e.g. "The soft young <u>down</u> of her; the <u>brown</u>".
inversion	Altering the <u>normal word order</u> for <u>emphasis</u>, e.g. "On the table sat a hedgehog."
irony	When <u>words</u> are used to <u>imply the opposite</u> of what they normally mean. It can also mean when there is a difference between <u>what people expect</u> and <u>what actually happens</u>.
juxtaposition	When a writer puts two ideas, events, characters or descriptions <u>close to each other</u> to encourage the reader to <u>contrast</u> them.
limited narrator	A narrator who only has <u>partial knowledge</u> about the events or characters in a story.

Glossary

linear structure	A type of narrative structure that tells the events of a story in chronological order.
linguistic devices	Language techniques that are used to have an effect on an audience, e.g. onomatopoeia.
list of three	Using three words (often adjectives) or phrases together to create emphasis.
metaphor	A way of describing something by saying that it is something else, e.g. "his feet were blocks of ice".
metre	The arrangement of stressed and unstressed syllables to create rhythm in a line of poetry.
monologue	One person speaking alone for a long period of time.
mood	The feel or atmosphere of a text, e.g. humorous, peaceful, fearful.
motif	A recurring image or idea in a text.
narrative	Writing that tells a story or describes an experience.
narrative viewpoint	The perspective that a text is written from, e.g. first-person point of view.
narrator	The voice or character speaking the words of the narrative.
non-linear structure	A type of narrative structure that tells the events of a story in a non-chronological order.
objective writing	A neutral, unbiased style of writing which contains facts rather than opinions.
omniscient narrator	A narrator who knows the thoughts and feelings of all the characters in a narrative.
onomatopoeia	A word that imitates the sound it describes as you say it, e.g. 'whisper'.
oxymoron	A phrase which appears to contradict itself, e.g. "pale darkness".
pace	The speed at which the writer takes the reader through the events in a text or poem.
paraphrase	Describing or rephrasing something in a text without including a direct quote.
parenthesis	A rhetorical technique where an extra clause or phrase is inserted into a complete sentence.
pathetic fallacy	Giving human emotions to objects or aspects of nature, in order to create a certain mood. E.g. "The fog stretched its cold fingers stealthily towards us".
personification	Describing a non-living thing as if it's a person. E.g. "The sea growled hungrily."
phonetic spellings	When words are spelt as they sound rather than with their usual spelling, e.g. "yow" instead of "you". It's often used to show that someone is speaking with a certain accent or dialect.
plosive	A short burst of sound made when you say a word containing the letters b, d, g, k, p or t.
protagonist	The main character in a text, or the leader of a particular cause or movement, e.g. Pip is the protagonist in 'Great Expectations'; Lenin was a protagonist in the Communist movement.
purpose	The reason someone writes a text, e.g. to persuade, to argue, to advise, to inform.
register	The specific language used to match writing to the social situation that it's for.

Glossary

rhetoric	Using language techniques (e.g. repetition or hyperbole) to achieve a persuasive effect.
rhetorical question	A question that doesn't need an answer but is asked to make or emphasise a point, e.g. "Do you think the planet is worth saving?"
rhyme scheme	A pattern of rhyming words in a poem, e.g. if a poem has an ABAB rhyme scheme, this means that the first and third lines in each stanza rhyme, and so do the second and fourth lines.
rhyming couplet	A pair of rhyming lines that are next to each other.
rhythm	A pattern of sounds created by the arrangement of stressed and unstressed syllables.
sarcasm	Language that has a scornful or mocking tone, often using irony.
satire	Text that makes fun of people or situations, often by imitating them and exaggerating their flaws.
second person	A narrative viewpoint that is written as if the reader is one of the characters.
sensory language	Language that appeals to the five senses.
sibilance	Repetition of 's' and 'sh' sounds, e.g. "a shrill whistle shattered the stifling silence".
simile	A way of describing something by comparing it to something else, usually by using the words 'like' or 'as'. E.g. "The apple was as red as a rose".
simple sentence	A sentence that is only made up of a single main clause.
slang	Words or phrases that are informal, and often specific to one age group or social group.
soliloquy	When a single character in a play speaks their thoughts out loud, but no other characters can hear them.
sonnet	A form of poem with fourteen lines, that usually follows a clear rhyme scheme.
Standard English	English that is considered to be correct because it uses formal, standardised features of spelling and grammar.
stanza	A group of lines in a poem.
structure	The order and arrangement of ideas in a text. E.g. how it begins, develops and ends.
subject	The person or thing that performs the action described by the verb. E.g. in "Billy ate a sandwich", Billy is the subject.
syllable	A single unit of sound within a word. E.g. "all" has one syllable, "always" has two.
symbolism	When an object stands for something else. E.g. a cross symbolises Christianity.
syntax	The arrangement of words in a sentence or phrase so that they make sense.
tabloid	A less formal type of newspaper, which often focuses on more sensational topics.
third person	A narrative viewpoint where the narrator remains outside the events of the story, written using words like 'he' and 'she'.
tone	The feeling of a piece of writing, e.g. happy, sad, serious, light-hearted.
viewpoint	The attitude and beliefs that a writer is trying to convey.
voice	The characteristics of the person narrating a poem or text.
volta	A turning point in a poem, when the argument or tone changes dramatically.

Index

Index

Index

Q

quatrains 54
question marks 75
quotations 4, 38, 44, 59, 61, 66, 69

R

register 11-13, 22, 23, 28
religion 12, 52
Renaissance 47
repetition 14, 18, 41, 49
reviews 33
rhetorical devices 11, 18, 28
rhetorical questions 18
rhyme 55
rhythm 55
Romanticism 52

S

sarcasm 17
satire 17
second-person narrators 19
semantic field 14
semicolons 75
sensory imagery 19, 56
sentence structures 21, 23, 36, 41
settings 37, 42
Shakespeare 36, 44, 47, 48
sibilance 57
silent letters 79
similes 15, 41, 56, 82
simple sentences 21, 81
slang 85
social class 12, 43, 51, 52
soliloquies 45
sonnets 54
speech
        used by characters 39, 41, 45
        delivering speeches 84, 85
        writing speeches 34, 84, 85
speech marks 77
spelling 74, 79
Spoken Language assessment 84, 85
stage directions 45

Standard English 35, 74, 84, 85
stanzas 54
stories (writing) 24-26
structure
        of exam answers 22, 60
        of fiction texts 20
        of non-fiction texts 20
        of poems 53, 54, 58, 61
        of prose and drama 42, 46, 49
style (of texts) 13, 46
summarising information 7
syllables 55
symbolism 42

T

tabloids 29
tenses 74, 80
tension 21, 24
tercets 54
themes 37, 43, 44, 59, 66, 67
third-person narrators 19, 21, 25, 30, 50
tone 13, 22, 23, 28, 30, 57
tragedies 47
travel writing 31

U

unseen poetry 53, 67-73

V

verbs 19, 80, 82
verse 44, 48
vocabulary 8, 25, 41, 63, 74, 82, 85

W

word types 80
writer's message 43, 67
writer's viewpoint 9, 12, 15, 28
writing style 13, 22, 23, 74, 81

EHR41